A Survival Kit
for the HEREAFTER

A Survival Kit
for the HEREAFTER

Belinda Silbert

DOUBLE
STOREY
a juta company

First published 2005 by Double Storey Books,
a division of Juta & Co. Ltd,
Mercury Crescent, Wetton, Cape Town

© 2005 Belinda Silbert

ISBN 1-77013-009-8

Editing by Olivia Rose-Innes
Page layout by Claudine Willatt-Bate
Cover design by Nic Jooste
Printing by CTP Book Printers, Parow, Cape Town

*For my mother Ann, who has birthed and
rebirthed me throughout my life; my three children,
Aviva, Sharon and Ross, who are my greatest
motivators; and in memory of my late father
Ralph Metlizky, an exceptional human who
did so much in his short life.*

CONTENTS

Introduction

We've all felt it at some stage: the exhaustion of a chaotic life, the suspicion that we're the butt of some cosmic joke. Perky lifestyle coaches tell us that when life gives us lemons we're supposed to make lemonade. Please. In the real world, when life gives us lemons we make strong coffee and try to get through the day without strangling someone.

Even capable lemonade-makers don't have all the answers. No matter how successful you are in your work, how happy you are in love, or how content you are with your family and friends, there is still that little hollowness that never goes away, a longing for something, a search for completion. It's like waking up alone on a tropical island: it's beautiful, the beaches are perfect, the sea is crystal clear and you have all the mangoes you can eat, but you don't know where you are or why you're there.

But there are answers, and that's what I hope this book will communicate. Answers about the soul and its survival after death; about empowering your life; about growing closer to God through realizing that there is so much more than there appears to be. Hamlet said it first and said it best when he recognized that there are more things in heaven and earth than are dreamt of in our philosophy.

Aren't there enough of these books? Why write another one?

There's a perception amongst the general public that this line of work attracts people who are failures in life. It's a cliché: the spinster with only a cat for company, sitting in a little kitsch flat, reading fortunes for emotionally damaged people. All you need is a trailer park next door and the bank repossessing the furniture, and you have what many people picture when they think of spiritual mediums and their clients. But the reality is that most of my clients are sane, successful people, coming to be empowered further in their lives.

Having said that, there are those who are weak or terribly vulnerable, who get addicted to readings, who will hitch their mind to any wagon that takes their fancy. This kind of person just cannot make a decision by themselves. The most common question I'm asked on the radio shows I do is: 'What must I do?' If you're asking that, you're already lost.

Let me put it this way. If you had a priceless antique, say a Ming vase that had been passed down to you through generations, would you hand it to some complete stranger you heard on the radio and let them fill it with who knows what? So why then would you hand over your mind, your most priceless possession of all? Why would you pass it from person to person, offering it to anyone whose opinion sounded plausible enough?

Often these people are joiners, workshop junkies who allow their lives to be dictated by worksheets and self-help gobbledygook, never internalizing the information they've been given and so always doomed to search for the quick fix to their problems. Only internalization can lead to growth. All true education is a question of internalized knowledge.

And education is what this book is about. It's not about

bringing comfort or evangelizing or getting my name in print. Without knowing where we came from and where we're going to, we can't function to our full potential. Potential is a word that's been overused by New Age gurus and those amazingly dull motivational speakers in cheap suits. It's come to mean the quest for a Volvo and a home in the suburbs. But for me potential refers to the spiritual, the capacity we all have as humans to evolve spiritually, which of course inevitably amplifies our emotional development.

How I know what I know

When I was very young, about three or four, I loved playing with other children. They were mostly strangers to me – I now think of them as extras on a movie set, faces in a crowd – but nonetheless I enjoyed their company. One little boy in particular was a favourite of mine, an 'extra' I called Dante Willy. I'd tell my mother that I was off to the park to play with Dante Willy, and off I'd go and talk about the things that are so important to small children, those conversations that are about nothing and everything. Dante Willy was a sweet and normal little kid, but one aspect of his life was not entirely ordinary: he said he'd been murdered in the park where we played.

Some psychics and mediums have written about their first experience of other worlds and often say how terrified they were when they first experienced otherworldly visions or paranormal events. Poor old Haley Joel Osment in *The Sixth Sense* always seemed to be teetering on the brink of a nervous collapse because of the 'dead people' he saw. But when you're four you often assume that your experience of the world is everyone's; in my case, I assumed that everyone plays with little dead boys in the park. It never even crossed my mind to be afraid.

As I matured and learned more about my skill, there were frightening times. Some spirits do try to scare you. Not the ordinary spirits who have passed over, but those still lurking in the lower astral. Now, I've been around the paranormal block a few times. I've been intimidated by thoroughly nasty spooks, had furniture flung at me, and even crossed as far into death as anyone living has a right to go, but when you're being targeted by a malignant force that knows exactly what fear buttons to push, only a fool or a liar would claim to be unafraid. For instance, one night after I'd attended an exorcism I woke up in bed, sensing a presence. Lying next to me under the covers, not three inches away, was the most disgusting old crone you could ever imagine. She manifested a sickly green light as she lay there. She didn't speak and she didn't move. She just lay in my bed and scared the living daylights out of me.

I also realized I had the ability to identify various diseases that Western medical science will confirm are invisible to the naked eye. By now even hardened sceptics and trained scientists recognize the existence of auras, the layers of energy that radiate from each one of us. For those who are able to see this energy, it appears as colours or patterns: a healthy body radiates a certain colour, and a diseased one similarly reveals itself. And it's not just serious illnesses like cancer or heart disease that radiate: even headaches and the common cold have their own unique form around the body.

Why I have this ability is anyone's guess. I suffer from temporal lobe epilepsy, so I'm sure a neurologist would tell you all this is a quantifiable symptom of my condition. I'll listen to his diagnosis with pleasure, but look at it from my point of view: it's tough to take a guy seriously when you can see his late mother lecturing him about being a smart alec, his great-grandfather chopping up brains on a candle-lit laboratory table in 19th-century France, and even his sexual fantasies.

Science will have to crunch the numbers and do the paperwork to catch up, but in the meantime I am positive about one thing: what I have is a gift from God. I have always felt close to God – He, She, It, it doesn't matter – and from early on I had a desire to become a rabbi, to minister to people and to tell them the good news about the Hereafter. Because the news is good. However, the reality of trying to bridge the gap between God and this world was more than I could cope with. To touch human horror and grief is a terrible thing, and takes a toll on one's mind and body that is uniquely awful; the agony of people who have lost a child is indescribable. I made the decision not to practise as a medium because I didn't want that constant exposure to suffering.

But with age and experience came the emotional maturity to deal with what I saw, and I realized that I could help in people's healing processes.

Why you paid for this book

You don't need to be a mind-reader to know what people think when they encounter a book like this or people who work in my field: dollar signs. Bereavement counselling? She's just cashing in on people's insecurities and pain. Guidance about the afterlife? It's a licence to print money!

I can understand people's suspicion. Psychics seem to have so much to say, but when the question of money arises they suddenly get tongue-tied, especially those who charge hefty appearance fees and are negotiating lucrative book deals.

But for me it's simple. I have to be compensated for what I do, the same as any other working person needs to be. Like more traditionally trained ministers of God I also have a congregation – all the people who have come and continue to come to me for guidance – and it's hard work, both physically and emotionally. It was a difficult decision to begin charging for my time and my ability, but one that was made easier by some people's insensitivity: having complete strangers phone at all hours, expecting me to dispense insights like some sort of mystic vending machine, wore thin very quickly.

Of course there are predators in this field, charlatans and hucksters who prey on the bereaved. They can't afford to offer closure to their victims, because closure for the heartbroken means cutting off a stream of easy money. (You don't even want to know the kind of karma that is piling up for these lowlifes ...) But somehow all psychics have been tarred with this brush, which is unfair and, frankly, uninformed. If I'm a predator, then psychiatrists and psychologists should be criticized too. Besides, you'll never find a genuine mystic sitting chewing on a pencil, making origami out of his patient's file, and saying 'Mmm, mmm, mmm, I see ...' for R300 an hour!

On the contrary, when people come to me I give them a plan of action, practical exercises that enable them to go out and take their lives forward. For me the acid test is that they don't come back to me week after week. Above all, it is one's responsibility as a mystic never to insult a client's intelligence. When you tell the bereaved something fluffy about heaven and angels and puppies in picnic baskets, you're doing them the gravest disservice you can: you're abusing their minds.

And now to begin. And in our case, the beginning is death.

1

Death and dying

Death just isn't what it used to be
I said that this book is not about bringing sentimental comfort to needy people, but it's inevitable that as we are slowly reminded of and reintroduced to our spiritual aspect, we gain the understanding that we are not as alone as we often feel in our daily lives. This discovery is far more comforting than someone (who knows no more than we do) telling us that all will be well, an opinion based on nothing but a hunch or blind optimism.

But with any discovery about life, or any process that involves examining how and why we live, we have to confront death and understand its central place in our world. This is not something most of us want to do, and it is a great pity that our culture and times have come between us and this crucial process. Death has got some pretty bad publicity in recent centuries, and today's Western society fears it more than ever before. We try to postpone it with visits to spas and plastic surgeons, with oxygen chambers and expensive torture in the guise of fitness regimes, shoehorning our wrinkly little bodies into lycra monstrosities and embarrassing our grandchildren wholesale. In fact when it comes to death we carry on like a bunch of children facing a visit to the dentist. We have entirely lost our ancient connections with death thanks to a culture that is obsessed with youth and fun.

We all know that life looks like a pair of brackets, enclosed on the one hand by birth and on the other by death; but for many people this fact – the reality of our mortality – is a terrifying prospect, and in our desperate efforts to stave off that little bracket, to keep it just beyond the horizon, we forget to live. An obvious example is the American pop icon obsessed with living like a child, whose numerous surgical procedures and reported experiments with rejuvenating chambers have left him looking like a desiccated corpse, with a life in ruins.

It's not just our own death that frightens us. We're also afraid of the dead. However much we miss and long for loved ones who have died, if we saw them again we would be terrified. What is this basic human fear, this terror of the dead? We don't seem particularly afraid of climate change or misplaced nuclear weapons, but we turn to jelly if we think we see the ghost of a dear grandmother or beloved husband! It's the great paradox of the living: it frightens us that we don't survive physical death, and it frightens us more that we might.

Ancient cultures on the whole did not share such fears. Certainly they feared the spirits of the restless or vengeful dead as much as if not more than we do, but they also understood death as a natural process, and recognized and embraced the need to help people make this transition.

Granted, some of these practices seem excessively literal to us today: however strongly you believe in the next life, you're not likely to demand to have your spouse, car, dinner service and CD collection buried with you. (At least I hope not, and if you are planning any of the above, please get help quickly.) But when a Viking warrior was pushed out into the fjord on his burning longship, surrounded by his trophies and weapons, those standing on the shore had no doubt that their departed hero was on his way to the banquet halls of Valhalla, and would need his possessions for when the great final battle of Ragnarok came, when the gods would all be killed and only a single man and woman would survive to start a new world.

The ancient Egyptians were no less exacting in their preparations, sending their dead rulers and noblemen into the next world with all their wealth and slaves. The Chinese, the Japanese, the Romans, many African cultures – all had a complex idea of the afterlife and its goings-on. Interestingly, many of these cultures separated the hereafter from the home of the gods: when Roman soldiers faced death, they did not believe they were going to drink ambrosia alongside Jove and Mars, but rather that they would wake up with all their fallen comrades in the Elysian Fields, an afterlife that closely resembled the landscapes of their mortal lives.

So precise and structured were the rituals of death for these cultures, that many codified them and wrote them down for future generations. Both Tibetan and Egyptian cultures featured a Book of the Dead, a kind of instruction manual – Everything You Ever Wanted to Know About Death but Were Too Afraid to Ask – and even the Jewish Kaddish follows similar lines, where prayers are said for the recently dead person in his or her transitional state.

This cornucopia of beliefs and rituals has come to be called 'mythology' by our culture. It's a word that is exotic and intriguing, but at the same time it denies reality. To us myths are events that never happened, and by herding ancient beliefs about death into the ghetto of mythology, we are saying that we do not believe in their possibility, their literalness. We prefer to talk of metaphor, parable, symbol, in our modern culture which does not believe in much apart from money and gratification. We deny those cultures their 'ironclad beliefs', and wait for science to give us our answers.

Perhaps this is where our fear comes from. We don't know. We don't know either way. We're embarrassed to tell people that we don't know. We're embarrassed if people claim to know. We can't understand an acceptance of death. In the Doge's Palace in Venice there is a magnificent room full of weaponry and pageantry from the Middle Ages. In one of the display cabinets is a suit of armour worn by a Venetian nobleman. It stands about five feet high, is pitch black, and pretty much how you'd imagine armour to look. Except for one horrible detail. It is covered in spikes, cruel six-inch spikes that jut out from the chest and knees and elbows. As modern people, many of us mercifully spared the horror of a major war in the last two generations, we cannot understand how a foot-soldier, armed with a pointed stick, could stay and face an onslaught by fifty of those spiked horrors on horseback.

The answer is belief. Firstly, people believed in their king or emperor or sultan, but secondly they had an unshakeable and very literal belief in the hereafter. Even in the 1600s, with the literalness of the holy texts of Christianity, Judaism and Islam already being questioned and attacked by scholars, ordinary people believed that this life is a brief moment of hardship before an everlasting reward. How else could you stand with your pointed stick, waiting for a certain and agonizing death?

With our loss of faith in God has come a loss of faith in death as a progressive experience, an evolutionary step. This book is intended to help bridge the gap between us and our relationship with the faith our forebears took for granted. In that respect, I like to think of it as a Book of the Dead for the 21st century.

Blasting off

To understand what happens when we die, we first need to understand that we are not just body and soul, or body and mind. In fact we are composed of a body, a mind and a spirit.

We are very familiar with our physical bodies, thanks to medical science, but we are less aware of our auras. 'Aura' is a term that has been trashed through its association with crystal-toting ex-hippies in tie-dyed sarongs, which is a pity because auras exist, and are clearly visible to many people, not just psychics or mystics. It was auras that I was seeing as a child, when I was able to diagnose various illnesses by looking at the specific patterns or colours displayed around people's bodies. Auras are energy, a physical extension of what's going on in our minds and bodies. You might not be able to see auras, but that doesn't mean people aren't emitting energy. You only need to hold your hand over someone's body to know that.

So the body and the accompanying energy field or aura are physical entities. We can measure and see these things. But around this physical body is an 'astral' body, which is how we leave our bodies when we die. It is in many ways similar to the physical body, but just exponentially less dense than flesh and blood. Some people believe you can actually calculate the weight of the astral body as it leaves, but understandably this hasn't been explored very far yet: emergency-room doctors are too busy tying off arteries and pulling out bullets to put their patients on scales and write down their findings.

Finally, around the physical body and the astral body we have the spirit body, which houses the soul. This can sound confusing, like almost-invisible Russian dolls inside very invisible Russian dolls, with a very visible Russian doll in the middle. But perhaps it's easier – and more appropriate, given what happens when we die – to think of an Apollo-mission rocket, waiting to launch at Cape Canaveral.

There's the launch-pad with its crude heavy gantries, the enormous bulky concrete slabs around the blast area, the control towers, the parking lots, and hundreds of kilometres of cable and pipe and wire to run the whole operation. That entire system represents your body. It's big, complicated, and not particularly efficient in terms of either energy or space.

The rocket itself is your astral body. It's sleek, vastly smaller and more nimble than the launch-pad and surrounds, but still weighs a ton or two. When you die – or, in our extended metaphor, the gantries fall away and the launch-pad finishes serving its purpose – the rocket fires up and takes over, and with sheer brute force blasts you away from the heavy pull of the earth.

But what happens to that rocket as soon as it has punched through the atmosphere? It is discarded, and either disintegrates or burns up. The astral body operates exactly the same way, disintegrating or peeling away as soon as we have entirely left the world of the living.

And so in the end we're left with the Apollo capsule, our spirit body, safely housing the little astronaut that is the soul.

So what does it feel like to die?

Because I can remember many of my past lives and past deaths, I know that what I most feared in other lifetimes was the moment when I stopped breathing. For me the cessation of breath has always been a fascinating and awful concept, because it seems to be so bound to the actual moment of death. I still don't know why this idea holds such sway over me, because I have long ago come to terms with the processes of death.

In the film *The Abyss*, the protagonists were able to operate underwater without oxygen tanks, thanks to a nifty liquid that they inhaled. This highly oxygenated substance was based on real research, in which rats were submerged – 'drowned' – in liquid with a very high oxygen content, and continued to live, if very uncomfortably. Imagine being presented with this substance, perhaps in a glass tank. Inhale it, drown yourself, and stop breathing air. And yet you continue to be conscious and aware of what is going on around you, despite the obvious confusion and mild panic triggered by the lack of air.

This is something like the moment of the last breath. But of course there is more to it. During a peaceful death (and one must be aware that there are many other kinds), either through disease or old age or sudden failures of the body like brain haemorrhages or heart attacks, there is a moment of absolute peace just before the final breath is snatched. 'Absolute peace' is a glib phrase, and it's worth taking a moment to imagine a state of complete contentment, with nothing outstanding or demanding a place in your mind and soul, with everything as it should be. It is stillness and quiet, alone but not lonely. People sometimes grimace at this point, at the moment of death, and we the living interpret this as a sign of pain or fear, but it is merely a muscular spasm, a reflex by the body to this entirely perfect moment.

Some people leave the body before it dies or before the last breath is taken. These spirits tend to float over the body, watching it and the events going on around it. Some of America's leading neurosurgeons have been doing groundbreaking work in this field, and science is slowly coming to the realization that 'out of body' experiences or 'near death' experiences are more than physical or chemical reactions. For years the vision of a tunnel with a bright light at the end, described by many people who have been brought back from the brink by medical science, was explained away as being caused by a lack of oxygen to the brain. Likewise, when people claimed to have seen the surgeon working on their unconscious bodies, it was suggested that their still-active brains had merely projected an imaginary scene into their minds.

But when certain patients emerged from brain surgery (in which almost all sensory functions are shut down) and were able to describe medical procedures or pieces of dialogue between surgeons, people sat up and took notice. There are neurological theorists who are now beginning to suggest that consciousness actually exists as matter at a subatomic level, and that when we go under the knife our consciousness can literally seep out of our bodies and hang in the air around or over us, recording events. When we come out of the anaesthetics, it is all drawn back into our heads, carrying its recording with it.

Now that's science's take, which is as usual limited by what can be proved outright. But what this is describing is the soul, observing its body in the point between life and death. Sometimes those souls return, sometimes they leave for the hereafter. Many people who have spoken about this inter-life experience, including the patients described above, have also said how bitterly disappointed they were at having to return. They resented having to go back to face a future of pain and rehabilitation. Most of all, they suddenly resented the limitations of the human body.

Interestingly, many doctors talk of the moment of death as something measurable only in the eyes of the dying person. Hardened surgeons, atheists to their core who regard people as engines of blood and bone, talk of a light going out in the eyes. It's not something measurable, or even visible most of the time. One moment there is a gleam of what we can only describe as life, and the next there is the dull stare of the eye as a lifeless organ. Some doctors have even tried to document this transition with photographs, but with no success. It is something that needs to be experienced. And it is at that moment, when the light goes out, that the soul has finally left the body.

Tunnel vision
What you see immediately after your death depends on what you need to see to be reassured. If you need to see angels coming to fetch you, they will appear. If you need to see Jesus Christ waiting for you with open arms, your first experience of death will be

a joyful and awe-struck reunion. If you don't have a particular preconception, and your soul has passed over to the next level and not gone to the astral level or purgatory, your family will come to fetch you. I'm sure some of us feel we'd rather wake up in hell than have our mad extended families fussing over us, especially family we don't know, but the compassion on the other side is so great that none of our worldly issues comes between us and their love. You will also not find it strange that the people embracing you are family that you've never met, people who lived long before you that you might not even have heard about. And yet they know you, and soon you will know them.

As for the tunnel with the bright light, it sometimes seems that everyone who is anyone has had a close run-in with it. But stereotypes don't come from nowhere, and the short journey through the tunnel is an almost universal experience of death. I doubt whether this tunnel really exists in space or time, even in the spirit world, but, significantly, it mirrors the birthing process that all humans have experienced, and it might be our way of interpreting the experience of our death in terms of our births, explaining it to ourselves as humans. This seems to be the case, since so many cultures feature the vision of a tunnel, whether they believe in one god or many, one afterlife or reincarnation.

The ways of dying

The experience of the moment of death is basically the same for everyone, but our reaction to it is as different as we are as individual humans. And just as the circumstances of our deaths are different from one another, the kind of death that we can experience has great variation.

The first distinction to understand is between deaths that are ordained and deaths that are not ordained. If something is ordained, it has been decided by a power greater than ours, and we have very little recourse for complaint.

An example of an ordained death is one that occurs as a result of illness. It is an act of God – not in the way the insurance companies mean, as in grand-pianos dropping out of the sky onto your Porsche – but also an act of nature, since the body that has died can no longer sustain the soul. If your death is ordained, you will be taken over very gently. If you have been suffering, either through dementia or pain or both, you will go to a 'place' – really a projection of your own mind – that seems like a hospital, where you will be able to adjust to the state of death.

Many people comfort themselves or others by saying that sudden deaths, regardless of the cause, were ordained. How often haven't you heard, 'Oh, but it was his time to die'? Often this is an emotional crutch for people who are not ready to confront their grief, or to question their relationship with God. For example, a family who loses children in a car crash often says that it was the children's time to die.

The truth is exactly the opposite. Most deaths resulting from some mechanical accident – car crashes, accidental shootings, industrial accidents – are not ordained. These deaths have not occurred because God decided they needed to: they have happened as a result of our species' abuse of power. More specifically, our abuse of the free will that allowed us to devise technology. I'm not advocating a Medieval attitude – don't go and drown your phone in the bath – but when we chose to make machines that could break and kill us, we opened the door to violent, premature deaths that were not ordained. So when people die in a plane crash, a train derailment, a car accident, it's a direct result of that decision. We've made the decision, not God, and so the deaths are not ordained.

The question of ordained and not ordained was one that tormented me when I was young. My father was 27 when he was killed by a drunken driver, and there was the chorus of 'Oh, it was his time to go'. But why, I wondered, was it his time to go when he'd only just blossomed into his full brilliance? He'd already done so much good, so why should all that potential have been snuffed out?

I realized that his death had absolutely not been ordained, but was a result of the abuse of technology (and alcohol). There was no decision or purpose in his death, no intention from either God or the drunken driver. I raged over that for some time until I understood the difference between the two kinds of death. And I also learned the unpleasant reality – one we all need to face – when someone experiences a death that is not ordained, they pass over traumatised, confused and angry.

Not that ordained deaths are necessarily peaceful, mind you. 'Do not go gentle into that good night,' urged Welsh poet Dylan Thomas. In his opinion, we should 'rage against the dying of the light'. And a surprising number of people share his view, despite undergoing ordained deaths. They pass over fighting all the way, not accepting death, tormented by fear of what is to come. They're furious, and manifest a kind of violence as they pass over – the kind of behaviour that would warrant a strait-jacket here in the world of the living.

These people are put into a sleep state so that they can wake up in something recognizable as a hospital, to help them to become more amenable. Imagine yourself being pulled into a situation in this life that frightened and confused you – someone rushing at you in an alley; a loud crash and then darkness; a strange noise and then an impact somewhere on your body. The next thing you experience is waking up in a hospital. At once you know:

something has happened to you
you are being cared for
you are safe
you won't be in bed for too long
you can expect jelly and custard at 4.30.

Okay, perhaps not the jelly and the custard, but you know all the rest just by opening your eyes and looking around. If you opened your eyes and saw someone on big feathery wings, playing a harp, you'd panic. The same applies to souls who have gone through fighting 'against the dying of the light'.

Of course I have no empirical evidence, but in my own experience the great majority of the dead go over in a confused state. Ordained, not ordained, peaceful, fighting – most do not know what is going on. Add to this the fact that most don't believe in life after death, and you've got a real epidemic of disorientation. Most people need to be counselled immediately, or in extreme cases even shown their bodies and have it all explained: you've had a quick death, a heart attack. You haven't been eliminated. It's okay.

If you expect your death, it doesn't mean you want to go when it happens. I had a case where a man was very sick, but he didn't want to die. He refused to come to terms with his death, and when it happened there was no closure. He went and examined his body at the funeral, and later saw it starting to disintegrate. It was a terrible trauma for him because he was still so attached to the physical realm of this life. It took him quite a while to settle on the other side.

If you haven't realized, in this life right now, that your body is not you, then your passage through death and to the other side is very difficult. It's worth repeating: *Your body is not you.* But if you have done the spiritual homework here, you'll go straight through. If you have children, you'll probably want to see how they are, and some people go to their funerals out of interest. But the difference between them and the man who fought all the way is that their interest is healthy, whereas he was obsessed.

It's not about believing in life after death, or being good or bad. It's about being ready to leave your body behind. I encountered an old lady who didn't have a strong belief in the afterlife at all. But she had been suffering terribly with illness in her last months of life, and when she died the relief was so overwhelming, and the release from her pain so wonderful, that she passed over without the slightest hiccup, as if she had been expecting it all her life.

Premature death

Accident, illness, suicide, euthanasia, abortion – all premature deaths but with their own specific circumstances and consequences. Abortion is the one that no doubt jumps out at you since this is such a contentious question today. I will discuss this issue shortly, but suffice it to say for now that aborted babies have experienced premature death. A life was truncated through an entirely human decision. What was ordained for that child? Who can say, but at the very least it had been ordained to be born.

Miscarriages are tragic, and because of the emotional suffering they bring to families one often encounters the familiar expressions of fate and ordination, the familiar emotional anaesthetic: five months was all that was given to this baby; its little time on earth had been completed; it was ordained by God.

My experience completely refutes this attitude, for the simple but crucial reason that I want everyone to understand and remember: *The human body is the wild card.* Our bodies are wonderful, but they're not perfect. Sometimes they can sustain the human soul, and sometimes they can't. There's nothing spiritually mysterious about this. A stillborn or miscarried baby might simply have drawn the short straw in terms of the little body it was given. Likewise the mother who carried it might just not have been able to give her child what it needed, through no fault of her mind or spirit or soul. Her body just didn't co-operate. It's awful to face, and we want to blame God or the universe for events like this, but we can't.

Another pernicious attitude that I often encounter, also an emotional crutch for the bereaved or their extended family, is that the dead child came to teach its parents something through its death. Little Alice drowned in the swimming pool so her parents could learn. It makes me crazy. Is that how to teach loving parents to keep a pool gate closed, by taking their only treasured child? These are not ordained deaths. These children didn't come into our lives to teach anyone anything. They came to live and enjoy their lives.

People who don't want to confront the wild card of the body also use this line of reasoning when a brain-damaged or re-tarded child is born to them. Children with Down's Syndrome are often extremely loving and placid, and their parents and rel-atives decide that their child came to them to teach them how to love, or how to accept things, or whatever. This is one way to deal with the struggle of having a disabled child, but it seems selfish. After all, the child's state is not about the parents, it's about the child.

And while on the subject of children with physical or mental disabilities, I wish people would stop referring to them as 'spe-cial'. All children are special. A child with mental disability is special, like all children, but he or she is also unfortunate. It wasn't meant to be, or ordained, or their karma, or a lesson for Mom and Dad. It's just plain unlucky.

Abortion

Only God's judgement carries any objective weight. So when I judge abortion to be murder, my judgement means as much or as little as you want it to mean. But I do know, from my contact with the next world and my experience of aborted souls, that doctors who perform abortions need to know that they are attracting the most hideous karma imaginable. It really doesn't get much worse. There is a well-known abortion clinic in Cape

Town, and I can't drive past it. The horror that reverberates out of that place is too much for me to handle.

My own attitude towards abortion has been shaped by being a woman, a mother and a Jew. Judaism says that the mother comes first. Until the child's head appears, the mother's life is paramount, to the point of doctors being entitled to cut the child out in pieces if it enables the mother to live. But as soon as the child's head emerges, the battle must be for both lives. The choice over which to save now rests entirely with the doctors, and the doctors must accept the karmic and spiritual repercussions of their decisions.

Technology has added another nasty wrinkle into the whole issue. For the first time as a species we can know if a child is badly damaged or disabled well before it is born. We cannot judge a parent who aborts a baby that would have had a painful and short life. But we must realize and accept that even that tormented parent has attracted a dark karmic burden. Certainly it is nowhere near as horrible as that attracted by a parent who terminates a perfect baby simply because a child would be an inconvenience. But we must recognize that there is judgement in the world. Not mine, not your mother-in-law's, but God's. I'm glad I'm not God, who knows how to judge between a destitute child-prostitute on the street who has an abortion, and a bored socialite who wants to keep her figure. Spiritually it would be wonderful to have a blanket ban on abortion. But is this realistic? I don't know. An acquaintance of mine who miscarried in Ireland nearly bled to death because the Catholic doctors would not perform an abortion and instead waited until nature took its course. This is neither sensible nor humane.

There does seem to be a kind of karmic sliding-scale. The decision to kill a child is judged according to motive and circumstances: there is compassion in the universe. But don't for a moment think that the aborted soul experiences anything other than terror and trauma. Before they die they experience the pain of what is often a brutal murder, and when they cross over they carry all the horror of that event. They go through screaming.

Doctors must be faced with these questions, and made aware of the consequences. Unfortunately the medical profession tends to attract people who have made an intellectual decision to prize science and ambition over the calls of the spirit and the subconscious, and even those who feel that abortion is wrong do not willingly explore why it is wrong. But in spiritual terms doctors are laymen, uninformed and ignorant, and they need to be told that to perform an abortion is to commit murder.

Recently when I was waiting to be helped at a surgery I glimpsed one of the resident doctor's business cards. The receptionist looked embarrassed and quickly covered it, saying I wasn't supposed to see it. But I had seen enough: he specialized in abortions. He has made a choice to enter an industry of death. I'm sure he has plausible-sounding explanations – it's a woman's right, if he didn't do it she'd have an illegal one and bleed to death – but by accepting money he's turned his surgery into an abattoir.

Not surprisingly, the souls of aborted babies can pass over harbouring immense resentment towards life in this world. They had made the decision to be born, had carefully assessed their parents and their potential, and then got butchered for their trouble. It's enough to make a soul very very bitter, and want to turn its back on this world for a long time.

In fact some aborted souls decide to 'grow up' on the other side, and not to reincarnate for some time. But some do feel strongly that they need to be reborn, and are not deterred by the trauma they've suffered. People who believe in reincarnation sometimes suggest that aborted children return to their families, the way miscarried children do.

This is rubbish. Would you go back to the people who killed

you before they'd even met you? In my experience this is one of the few absolutes in death and the Hereafter: aborted babies avoid their original families like the plague.

It's bitterly ironic that when the issue of abortion comes up in public debate or in the media, it is often repeatedly linked with one word: 'sensitive'. It's a *sensitive* issue, it must be handled *sensitively*, the state is *sensitive* to the rights of women. What a terribly inappropriate word for the most insensitive act in the world.

Alzheimer's and other dementias

The death of people suffering from dementias is generally not traumatic; in fact it is almost always a blessed relief. It has been very well documented how Alzheimer's sufferers gradually start blurring reality and old memories of times past: they seem to have no problem recognizing photographs of people from their early childhood or teenage years, people perhaps long dead, but their spouses and children appear to them as complete strangers.

Memories begin to push our reality out of the consciousness of an Alzheimer's sufferer. Our reality, the events and sensations of this year or this week, becomes increasingly meaningless to them, while their memories become more 'real' than the people in the room around them. In the final days of their lives, this apparent loss of reality becomes literally real: they are visited not only by people from their past but by people from their future. These are souls coming to help them across the transition of death. To the dying person, it seems like another one of their fantasy-reality dreams, and there is no trauma at all. On the other side they are nursed and counselled, as if nothing has changed, but slowly they become aware of their new state, and they regain the focus of a soul unhindered by the mental ailments of the living.

A disease like Alzheimer's is purely a physical event. It has no karmic or spiritual origin. It is not a punishment for past misdeeds, or a lesson for the family of the sufferer. It is simply the old wild card – the body or, in this case, the brain malfunctioning. Mercifully it is a peaceful death. Strokes, on the other hand, are awful. Victims of strokes are trapped in their heads. They want to die, but they don't know how to die, and worst of all, they can't communicate with their families. That's when it can be useful to call in a medium to find out what a person's wishes really are.

Suicide, euthanasia and martyrdom

So often we feel angry when someone takes their own life. It's as if they've broken something precious, or wasted a valuable gift. When that waste takes innocent people with them, our anger turns to outright rage or hatred. And that anger doesn't come from nowhere: it's an accurate reflection of how suicide is seen by the greater powers of the universe. After all, it's still murder, even if it's self-murder.

The experiences of death are no different to those discussed above – confusion or trauma, relief and peace – but unlike other deaths (where the dying soul is not in control of the process) suicide brings with it severe consequences in terms of karma and spiritual trauma, and it is in these terms that suicide should be discussed.

First I must distinguish between suicide and assisted suicide, or euthanasia. Suicide, that which attracts such dark karma, is the taking of one's own life out of selfishness or weakness, or emotional anguish. Euthanasia, which brings relief to people suffering physical pain, is not suicide and as such carries almost no karmic baggage. I'm still waiting for someone to explain to me why doctors who perform euthanasia are prosecuted while those who do abortions are not …

To commit suicide you need to be in a pretty bad way, but don't expect any sympathy in the Hereafter. Even those who take their lives because their minds collapse, who 'snap', face purgatory. The reason for this is simple: if you're confused and deluded enough to kill yourself, to ignore the realities of the grief you are about to inflict on those who love you, then you're mightily confused and deluded. So why should that confusion and delusion just disappear as you die? Your mind and persona are not erased as you die: suicide brings no relief from self-loathing or confusion. All that mental anguish and moral numbness simply goes with you, heightened by what is almost always a traumatic death, and you go straight to the place that best reflects your thoughts and emotions: the Grey Zones, or, more bluntly, purgatory.

But as I will keep saying in this book, there is compassion in the universe, and the soul who has killed himself or herself in a moment of madness is judged less harshly than the one who has plotted and schemed over the event for months. Those who have planned their deaths will stay in the Grey Zones, the slumlands, for some time, but they will eventually look up to see the light and compassion of God, and begin their journey towards that light. Of course there are those people who kill themselves solely to hurt a spouse or lover, leaving bitter and accusing notes behind, and in terms of what's waiting for them, let's just say they won't be going on any journeys anytime soon.

Discussions about suicide nearly always include Catholicism. Even non-Catholics will know that this church believes suicide to be a mortal sin, an act as heinous as murder, and one that sends you straight to the cosmic penitentiary. So what happens to those few devout Catholics who do commit suicide, driven by mental imbalances or a particularly horrible set of circumstances? They're expecting to be plunged into a traditional pit of fire, populated by demons waving kebab-skewers and nasty whips. Sounds like an average braai in Benoni. But I digress. What will these miserable souls encounter?

Simple. They'll be dragged into a hellish inferno, with all the demons and pitch-forks they could ever wish for. Because that's what they have wished for. Hell is an illusion, a representation of internal agony, and so when they enter the Grey Zones they will experience what they expect to experience. But if they believe that they are in hell rather than purgatory, in other words in a place of eternal damnation and no hope, it will take far longer for them to realize that there is a way out, that they are in a grim lobby rather than locked in a black cellar for eternity.

In complete contrast to the bleak consequences of suicide is the release provided by euthanasia. In my experience of souls who pass over through assisted suicide, the question of murder or karmic retribution never even arises. People suffering from AIDS or other tormenting and terminal diseases who have found a way of killing themselves go straight to the next level: I've never encountered a single soul who has been relegated to the Grey Zones for dying in this way. They've gone straight to relief and the new life of the Hereafter.

Likewise I've never been given any reason to think that those who assist with euthanasia, be they doctors or the children of dying parents, are judged harshly.

Euthanasia is controversial and has been in the news for the last few decades, but it's a tea-party compared with the issue of martyrdom, by far the most controversial form of suicide, and still hotly debated today as it was 2000 years ago. But in karmic terms, it's as simple as black and white.

Someone who walks onto a crowded bus or into a busy café with a bomb strapped to them is fully aware that they are about to commit murder. In fact, that is the main point of the mission – their own death, or martyrdom, is merely an added bonus in their mind. This is premeditated mass murder, and it carries an extremely heavy price in the Hereafter.

It is this intention that makes all the difference. If you decide that your cause is best served by blowing yourself up or setting yourself on fire without harming anyone else, your stay in purgatory will be relatively short, a mere inconvenience on your path towards God.

A fascinating illustration of martyrdom's penalties is found in the legend of the Jews at Masada. A group of Jewish rebels had occupied the mountain fortress of Masada, refusing to submit to Roman rule and face trial for murdering other Jews whom they considered Roman sympathizers. A Roman legion was dispatched to the barren desert at the foot of the huge flat-topped rock, and, seeing no easy way up, began to build an enormous ramp up towards the fortress.

Soon it became clear to the Jews at the top that the Romans would complete their ramp in days, and would take the fortress in a matter of minutes once they reached the top. According to the legend, the Jews drew lots and killed each other and their families rather than face the possibility of being captured and sold into slavery. New archaeological evidence has cast doubt on the accuracy of the original story, but either way, some men did kill their wives and children, and then themselves.

Throughout the 1960s and 1970s this story was used as a rallying-cry for Israeli patriotism, until people began to suggest that it didn't make much sense to use a massive defeat as a nationalistic emblem. Also, devout Jews pointed out, suicide is one of the worst sins in Judaism.

And they were right. Yes, the Romans might have killed the defenders anyway, but the only one who can make a decision about taking a human life is God. The Jews of Masada were entitled to make the choice to take their own lives. But they had no right to make that choice for their children.

It's a terrible situation, and please God you and I are never placed in one similar. If you're in a burning skyscraper with your child, do you give her sleeping pills to save her the horror of jumping or burning to death? Without thinking about it carefully, we feel that this would be the right thing to do, the merciful thing to do. But there are harsh spiritual consequences waiting for us: children's lives are not ours to take. In the end the only choice we have is to fight to save their lives until we ourselves die.

Next stop, Hereafter

Death is forever, right? Not if you've read this chapter. Death is a twinkling of an eye, a little bump in the road. An important, crucial bump, but just a bump nonetheless. Death doesn't mean anything without what comes before and what comes after. And what comes after, comes next. Next stop: the Hereafter. Where it all begins.

The Hereafter

Are we going home?

'Swing low, sweet chariot, coming for to carry me home!' So sang American plantation slaves, longing for a death that would unite them with God, and, as importantly, give them the home they had never known in the generations since they were torn from their African motherland. The Hereafter, heaven, paradise, was the ultimate reward but also the Promised Land, a home-land.

When Jesus Christ taught acceptance of diversity he used a metaphor of home: 'In my father's house there are many rooms.' It was a metaphor with powerful resonance, and to this day, regardless of the God and scriptures they follow, people look to the place after death as their eternal home, where they will be welcomed, loved and secure.

What makes home so special, so comforting? Perhaps its strongest pull on our hearts and minds is that it is a destination, something that we return to when our life's journeying is done, somewhere we won't have to leave again. We resist change. Movement, either physical or emotional, is at least uncomfortable, at worst traumatic. It's only natural that we think of the Hereafter as a permanent home.

The result of this kind of instinctive thinking – or is it instinctive hoping? – is a view that is common to most religions: that the Hereafter is the whole point of our existence, and that our lives on earth are merely a brief wait at the bus stop of the universe.

But the reality is different.

When you were five or six, did you think of older people simply as Big or Grownup? Fifteen-year-old siblings, thirty-something people you saw around you, parents of friends: all looked the same. You were Small, and they were Big, and that was that. You also knew that if you were good and brushed your teeth twice a day and ate your vegetables, you would be Big one day too. You never gave this much thought – it was just something that would happen at some stage. One week you would be Small, and maybe the next week you'd be Big.

Traditional views of the Hereafter are much like our childhood ideas of growing up. One day, we learn, we will be mortal people, flawed and confused, and the next we will be souls in heaven (or hell!) for all eternity. Heaven if we've brushed our spiritual teeth twice a day and eaten our moral vegetables; hell if we've been chomping chocolate bars and boozing. One day Small, the next day Big.

So if we're not home when we get there, where will we be?

The Seven Heavens
My belief, and that of the Kabbalah, is that there are seven heavens. You'd be forgiven for picturing a sort of divine wedding-cake, each layer a little higher, each with slightly more marzipan and an extra twirl or two in the icing. But of course these heavens aren't 'higher' than each other, since heaven – indeed, everything that lies beyond our own little world – has no physical

space. And each one isn't 'better' than the last: this is a moral concept, one that implies earthly standards and norms. All one can say with any certainty is that each level is closer to God, and closer to the soul's final reunion with God.

What does it mean to be reunited with God? The traditional religions of the world teach their followers to believe in an earthly interpretation of the idea of reunion: they will die and, if found worthy, will go to heaven where they will live forever, individual souls basking in the glory of the God they worship. If they've been especially righteous, they hope to be invited to sit at the right hand of God (or at least somewhere near His right foot, if they're suitably modest!) – a very physical and literal interpretation.

Perhaps the early prophets and saints who experienced divine enlightenment had a more abstract view. Perhaps to them paradise or heaven was all part of God's consciousness. But thousands of years of re-translation, and interpretations by people with not much education or sensitivity to symbolic language, have given modern humanity this idea of God sitting in a garden, with us around Him, together but each of us unique.

'Reunion' literally means 'become one again'. How can we become one with God if we're sitting at his right foot or swanning about in paradise? Hence the notion of the reunion that lies beyond the seventh heaven is one that many people find intimidating at best, frightening at worst. Because when we finally reach God, we are absorbed. His energy, that sun that created all suns, the heat and light of all possible universes, takes our souls into it and makes us become nothing and everything. We are obliterated in order to become part of that enormous consciousness, that enormous love. We disappear and are no more.

Obviously this is not a very palatable thought to us. Our modern world prizes individuality (to a certain extent: this will be mentioned again in the section on the Occult), and our very sanity leans heavily on our existence as unique, independent people. Think of all the Hollywood blockbusters that draw on this fear of ours, from implanted memories to drones living in the Matrix to a giant televised reality show that we believe to be real life. We are thrilled and awed by these disturbing ideas, safe and warm in the knowledge that we are us, that one plus one is two, and that Bob is Bob and not Louise or a figment of some cosmic joker's imagination.

It seems infinitely petty and ungrateful to reassure you about this final fate that awaits our souls: after all, our ascension to pure godliness should be something we celebrate and work towards. But let me say, if you're suddenly feeling a little queasy about the whole destruction-of-self thing, that by the time we reach the fourth or fifth levels of heaven, banal little human issues like these seem very far away and completely irrelevant to us.

The idea of seven heavens, or seven levels of one great heaven, has got some bad press in recent centuries. Orthodox Christianity, Judaism and Islam have frowned on the notion, instead offering their followers an immediate transformation and a reunion that is more satisfying to the human ego. You yourself might have felt a little twinge when you read the heading above, suddenly suspecting that you were unwillingly being led down a path that ends in crystals, sweat-lodges, soy-milk and clothing made of sacks. But the implications of my belief are immense, and offer even the most traditional follower of those faiths confirmation of God's immensity, of His compassion, and of our eventual path towards Him. Call it salvation, anointing, righteousness, whatever phrase your church uses – it's all the same thing. The only difference is that it takes that much longer to get there, and the journey contains more learning and experiencing than we could ever believe possible.

I'm sure some of the scepticism and intolerance levelled at the concept of seven heavens stems from the over-exposure of the number seven. To us in our sophisticated cynical world, it probably seems a little too 'mystical', like the number thirteen. I can quite understand how cynics would smell a rat or sense yet another spiritual quick fix punted by charlatans.

In fact I have no idea why there should be seven heavens and not three or nine or forty-six. The number seven has always been a powerful one in human society, whether we as a species gave it that power or whether it was intrinsically powerful from the beginning. After all, God created the world in six days and rested on the seventh, so why wouldn't He want to make His first holiday a special number?

I'm being facetious of course, but the fact remains that I can't claim any certainty about the number. In my own family it has been a terribly unlucky number, but one can't deny that it seems to exert some sort of pull on us, like the numbers one or three or thirteen, for reasons we can't quite explain.

Of course I hope that we discover more about these numbers and their significance, whether through the research of mathematicians and physicists (who are increasingly moving closer towards the divine mysteries so long denied by scientists), or the work of mystics and philosophers. Perhaps I, and people like me, can help in this regard; but of course now I'm talking like a modern human, needing the approval of science before I can wholeheartedly believe something to be true.

Which is not to say that research, be it scientific or esoteric, is not important. Nothing gets my back up like uneducated people (or those brandishing a certificate from Madame Zoltar's Cosmic Academy of Instant and Cost-Effective Enlightenment) who tell me that the mysteries of the universe are eternal, or that we shouldn't ask questions that are beyond our understanding. Some things, these quacks say, aren't meant to be understood by us.

What a load of bull. We have brains and logic and insight for a reason, and I have absolutely no doubt that the secrets of the universe and our place in it are waiting to be laid bare by hard spiritual and scientific work. Besides, you can't have it both ways: you can't say that God made us perfectly, and at the same time insist that we should remain ignorant of things we are equipped to decipher! That's just stupid. But then so are a lot of people who are too lazy to tackle these problems for themselves …

I get very frustrated by cultures that have allowed their priests or mystics to keep knowledge secret. For instance there are archaic cultures in which men have knowledge that they may not share with women. Of course, for 'may not' read 'will not for fear of being made obsolete'. For millennia, shamans, gurus, swamis, monks, mystics, visionaries, imams, rabbis and Popes have kept their knowledge exclusive, and this can only have set us back as a species. Imagine if scientists of the Enlightenment or Industrial Revolution had kept their discoveries limited to a few furtive meetings in secret corridors, whispering in code to each other about steam engines and penicillin?

That's why I believe it is my duty to share what I know, and I hope that this sharing may bring us closer to some understanding of the structure of the unknown and invisible universe.

Good vibrations

It is important for me at this point to explain some of the 'geography' of the spiritual universe.

We all know where we stand, literally speaking. Every year astronomers peer deeper into the universe, looking for more stars to add to the handful we know about. We know about moons and solar systems and galaxies, and some seriously clever people are hard at work figuring out the history and future of our universe, and whether there are more like it. Much of our experience of our world is very concrete: we feel and smell and touch and see our world. It was a very human act to bring rocks back from the moon, a tangible piece of another small world.

But some of what we know around us is less concrete. For instance, we can't see ultra-violet rays that burn our skin, or microwave frequencies that carry our television and radio signals. We know they're there, because we have instruments that can detect them, but otherwise in a strange way we're going on faith.

You've also probably seen a picture of light broken down into its various frequencies, a spectrum of colours representing different wavelengths. Again, our experience of light is simple and crude: blue is blue and red is red, and at night it all goes a rather nice shade of dark purple.

So we accept that our world and universe are full of frequencies and waves, pulses and particle showers that we cannot see, hear, touch, taste or feel. But the reality is there are far more of these frequencies and energies, far more variations and subtlety, than humans are able to detect with scientific instruments. Even now entire universes surround us that we can't experience, universes filled with energy and souls and action that are totally unreachable by us because they are on a different frequency. They are not light years away, or in other universes sitting next to ours. They are here, around us, between you and that tree over there; between earth and our moon, everywhere.

Here's an analogy that might make this clearer. Have you ever met someone so strange and alien to you that they almost seem unreal? Consider two people, one a hyperactive ultra-ambitious fashion model, the other a retired widower who collects butterflies. They have nothing in common except where they live (our planet), they don't know each other (and wouldn't want to), and if they passed in the street the chances are that they literally wouldn't see each other. If asked to describe the relationship between these two people, what would you answer? 'They live in different worlds'? 'They're not on the same wavelength'?

35

Two very common expressions, and both more accurate than we know.

So where is this next level that we're talking about? It is all around us, inside us, over us. It exists everywhere, because it is simply a higher vibration. And there are lower vibrations, too, the dark region of the astral which I will talk about shortly. Neither affects us in our daily lives. Neither can touch us in a physical way. Usually the inhabitants of these realms have no power to appear to us or reach us in any way. Like a huge crowd hurrying along a city pavement, where everyone is lost in their own thoughts and ambitions, we surge along together and past and across each other, perhaps sensing that we are not alone but too focused on our own lives – our own frequency – to have any contact with other souls.

Cars and shopping malls?

When we die we are not going home. We are not going to heaven. We are not going to a heavenly garden. We are not going to a golf estate in Florida. We are simply crossing into the first of those seven heavens, which for clarity I'll refer to as the first level.

We're no strangers to this realm. We've been there before. In fact we came from there, when we chose our parents from what is a fairly good vantage point onto our physical world. It's only natural that we return there. Many psychic or spiritual writers describe a hierarchy of spiritual worlds, which I endorse, but they go on to suggest that our earth, this noisy little ball on which we live, is fairly advanced in that hierarchy. In other words, we've already come a little way along the path when we are born into this world.

Only a comfortable, well-fed professional Western mystic could come up with something that fatuous. You only have to step outside the air-conditioned restaurant, to take a nervous taxi ride through the squalor and misery that torments the vast majority of our species, to know that this world is as low as it gets in spiritual terms. It has sorted nothing out, found no answers for itself. It is a bewildering soup of good and evil, order and chaos, hope and despair. There's nothing 'advanced' about either this world or us who inhabit it.

By now most people will have heard the views of famous psychics on what the Hereafter looks like, and frankly it sounds about as fun as licking gravel. If you were hoping for rain-forests teeming with all the beautiful life of earth, or secret gardens with stone walls dripping with honeysuckle and bumble-bees, or thunderclouds a thousand metres high over cliffs above sapphire seas, you're going to be disappointed. Because the Hereafter, according to many of these people, is full of cars and shopping malls.

But perhaps I'm being unfairly harsh, and I should explain why the psychics who have provided these mundane descriptions have done so.

In the previous chapter I described how the dead are confused by the experience of dying, and whether their death is peaceful or traumatic, they all have a sense of disorientation, sometimes even panic. And I said how God – or more accurately the process that was set in motion by God – eases that confusion by presenting the dead with images they can understand and process: a family member leading them through the tunnel, relatives meeting them on the other side, and so on.

What we find on the first level after earth is determined in the same way. We have come out of a concrete, literal world, where gravity, time, light and heat all have an effect on us. We have crossed over worrying about those we leave behind, perhaps grieving over the pain our death has caused them. We are still living very much in the 'real' world, despite the fact that we have died.

And so, because the universe as a whole is compassionate, we are given an image that will cushion the shock, a world in which we will be able to cope, emotionally and psychologically. In other words, we get what we expect to get, and what we need to get. Imagine if you can that you have experienced a traumatic death. As with a bad injury in this life, when you regain your consciousness you just want to lie still in your own bed, looking out of the window at a familiar tree or street, or reading a favourite novel. You don't want to be soaring on golden wings over a desert of pearls or talking to Alexander the Great or any of the other things that we're traditionally supposed to do in heaven. It's exhausting just thinking about it.

As we in the industrialized West move further and further away from the realities of suffering and disease and poverty, our emotional experience of the world becomes more and more limited. And in turn our understanding or expectations of the afterlife become more limited. To the slaves who sang 'Swing Low', death would bring freedom, love, the River Jordan and the land of milk and honey. To Muslim devotees, Paradise beckons. But to many in the West that bright light is dimming.

The concept of heaven has meant many things to many people, but until recently it was depicted in Western art and literature as a wild and fantastical country, with magnificent bluffs and waterfalls and fields of flowers under great clouds. The artists of the Enlightenment saw it as an awesome city, reflecting their hopes and belief in order and civilization, with arches and boulevards and fountains; Rome and London and Paris all rolled into one, without the dirt or crime or poverty.

It's only natural, I suppose, that people whose experience of this world is one of suburbia, and who have aspired to nothing more beautiful or profound, will encounter suburban scenes in the Hereafter. What we find is a representation, one largely created by ourselves.

Which raises fascinating questions about objective beauty. If someone had lived their whole life in a ghastly slum and never seen anything beautiful, not even a postcard of a beach or a glimpse of beauty on television, would they pass over into a slum-type environment (which seems pretty unfair!) or is there some higher objective beauty in store for them?

The good news is that beauty is not in the eye of the beholder. It exists, created by God outside of humanity and our world, and that person would encounter as much beauty as they could deal with, and the kind of beauty that would have an effect on them. In other words, instead of living in a slum they might find themselves in their ideal little town or city, inhabited by loving, curious people, with public spaces that struck them as beautiful. We already have an example of objective godly beauty on this earth in the form of music, which comes from higher realms. Consider the music of Bach or Mozart, or even composers of the 19th and 20th centuries, both classical and popular: to create beautiful music, or any music at all, while in the midst of war and violence and poverty and political upheaval, is a reflection of the divine objectivity of beauty. It comes into this world like a sunbeam into a dark room.

Another interesting example is that of insane people who pass over. If we experience what we expect to experience, or create a representation with our minds, surely the insane would find themselves in a heaven full of chaos and fear, populated with the full range of nightmarish and bizarre creations, both kind and sadistic?

Certainly this would be the case, but where 'sane' souls experience a period of rest and acclimatization in something resembling a rest-home or hospital, these poor souls are literally knocked flat, put in what I can only describe as a divine sanatorium, and wiped clean the way you would a blackboard or videotape. As anyone who has dealt with mentally damaged or defective people will know, there is usually nothing wrong with their souls: it is merely their human brain, their earthly hardware, that is malfunctioning. All of that is removed as they die, and they emerge as ordinary souls, no longer tormented or limited.

Of course you might ask: what about those who only think they're sane? Could they slip the net? Could there be paranoid schizophrenics wandering about in the Hereafter? And the answer to that is yes. God doesn't work in the Hereafter, He only set the basic machinery in motion. So it is absolutely possible that there are those who got through, and who will have to discover their condition in time. Everything is discovery.

The world we see around us in the Hereafter seems very real, and it serves a very profound purpose, but these manifestations or representations are only necessary for as long as the soul needs them. When we die and pass over to the first level of the Hereafter, we need the comfort and reassurance of a kind of physical reality; but on the second and third levels there is no scenery, no physical representation at all. Again this sounds rather dull, but by the time we get there (if we are determined and responsible enough to get there at all!) we don't need a visible or tangible environment.

Not everything is just a projected creation of thought, though, on the first level. When we imagine ourselves in the Hereafter we naturally picture ourselves in a body, with two arms and two legs. If fact you're probably hoping you're going to find yourself in a body with fantastic muscle tone, a washboard stomach and a head of shampoo-commercial hair to top it all off, flicking back and forth in some conveniently playful divine breeze …

We create this picture for ourselves because it's very difficult to imagine what a free-flying soul looks like, but the reality is not too different from our imaginings. Remember about our spirit bodies and the analogy of the rocket on the launch pad? It is that spirit body (invisible and immaterial in this life) that we 'wear' on the other side.

Of course there are also those who are unable to leave the earth plane with its material properties, because they can't come to terms with the idea that they have died. Sometimes they can't cross over because they are addicted to earthly things or material possessions. These souls remain in their astral body, and they are what we know as ghosts. Imagine our rocket, unable to get into space (because it is held back by the heavy weight of earthly desires), and instead it orbits high in the sky, round and round, leaving its trail among the clouds with an ominous rumbling sound. It's an unsettling thought, but then ghosts have always unsettled us. But I digress ...

Who do we meet on the other side?
Remember, everything we experience in the first few timeless moments after death (perhaps a millisecond, perhaps a decade: it doesn't matter) is adapted to what we can deal with psychologically and emotionally. So the simple answer to that question is: we meet who we are able to meet.

The newly dead soul is certainly not mobbed by a gang of ancient relatives, burying him or her under an avalanche of cupcakes and flowers of condolence. Only those who will ease the transition, or are familiar, will be there to meet the new arrival: perhaps a parent or a loved grandparent, perhaps a sibling. However, even those dearly loved people are sometimes too much to process. If you still haven't understood that you have died or that you have crossed over into another existence, seeing a long-dead parent would be tremendous shock and probably just worsen the trauma and heighten the sense of disorientation. In this case you might be approached by someone you don't know, but who seems to know about you, and who clearly cares about you: you will not know for some time that this person is a great-aunt you never knew, or an ancestor from centuries ago.

A question I'm sure you've often asked yourself (and one that sceptics love asking me!) is this: what happens if you've loved three people in your life, say over the course of a lifetime? Who do you end up with in the afterlife? What if you've married seven people? It's a natural question to ask, but only because tradition-al religion has told us that the Hereafter is fixed and eternal. But settling down and living happily ever after is the last thing that goes on in the next life: the Hereafter is about learning and mov-ing on, either by returning to this world to grow further, or by moving on down the path that leads closer to God.

So yes, you're likely to meet people you've loved, but not nec-essarily as soon as you die. They might be elsewhere (back on earth, reincarnated, or in other heavenly planes), and it might be seconds or millennia, in our crude way of measuring time, before you bump into them again. This is why I don't believe in the popular concept of soul-mates: in the end our only soul-mate is God, and we cannot be bound to another soul when we both still have so much to learn, and so much to experience in different and separate directions.

So what now?

As I've described in the last chapter, the first thing most souls do when they pass over is rest. They rest in a world – a projection of their own expectations and needs – that is very familiar and reas-suring. Perhaps they find themselves in a version of the house they lived in when they were a child, a happy place filled with security and love and wonder. Perhaps it's a flat overlooking a park, a vantage point to watch people coming and going down below. Perhaps, for those not passing over from Western cultures, it is a hut on a hill, or a little homestead on a plain.

It is the kind of place where one could happily do nothing for an eternity. There are the cool breezes and gently flapping curtains that talk of endless holidays, a lifetime of rest and meditation, and perhaps, one day, a slow decision to start doing something slightly more active.

So why do we just want to snooze or look out of the window as soon as we arrive at this place, when the purpose of death and our progression through the seven heavens is growth that allows the soul to learn about itself and find God?

The answer is simple and very familiar to all of us alive today: laziness. We're bone idle! Left to our own devices we tend to grind to a standstill. We work and learn because we have to, not generally because we want to. But even those rare and admirable people who work out of self-motivation and who exude energy often reveal the greatest laziness of the type that we're all guilty of: spiritual laziness. Finding our own truths, learning who we are, searching for God; all are difficult and often unrewarding in the short term, and so we shrug and give up. Laziness often gives rise to the most creative and naughty excuses, and I'm sure you've used one of these on yourself at some time or another. It's too hard, which means I'm over-thinking it, which means I'm not going by faith, so I should wait for a sign. I'll wait until I'm older and more mature. I'll figure these things out when I have children. I'll work on this if I get terminally ill. God loves me just as I am. There is no God, so why worry?

Because of all this procrastination, the great majority of those who die have not come close to doing the kind of spiritual work – divine aerobics, for want of a better metaphor! – necessary to evolve into a higher being. Spiritually they are in exactly the same place they were ten minutes earlier when they had a heart attack or stepped in front of a bus. It's really pretty logical: why should a stopped heart or broken body magically give us deep insight, or automatically dropkick us onto a higher level of enlightenment?

It takes a dramatic and profound experience to shift these souls out of their comfort zones. You know from your own life how difficult it is to energize someone who just wants to loaf: parents of teenage boys will know the agonies of trying to get his egotistical, volatile and self-pitying backside up off the couch! And you'll know that talking usually has absolutely no effect. You can talk until you hyperventilate and fall over, but that friend, that relative, that surly pimply lout in front of the TV – all basically ignore you.

So what do you do, in your own life? At least, that is, after you've yelled and screamed and slammed doors? The chances are that you find a way to *show* the person the error of their ways, to illustrate or demonstrate how you think they are going off track. It's the first law of creative writing, and it works just as well in everyday life: show, don't tell.

And the next level of our soul's existence operates in exactly the same way. Instead of having a family member or an angel or a spirit guide coming to our bedside and giving us helpful suggestions – 'You should get out more often, join a book-club!' – we are energized and jolted in a way we could never have imagined possible.

Imagine being able to re-enter your life in this world, but this time as an invisible observer. Like Scrooge witnessing his life with the Ghosts of Christmas Past, Present and Future, every spirit in the next world must quite literally face the lives that they have lived. Regardless of how peaceful or traumatic our crossing was, or how good or nasty we were in this life, we all experience the same profound overview of our lives. Every moment, every thought, every action of our lives is displayed to us in this ultimate interactive display. You watch, objective and often a little appalled. Is that me? Did I do that? How could I have said that? But you can't turn away, and you don't want to turn away. Not that you could: this entire process happens in an instant, like a wave of recognition and memory washing over you as fast as thought.

It is a sobering experience, but also vastly empowering and energizing. You have probably already experienced something a little similar in this life: a moment of clarity, a sudden objective realization about some aspect of your character or behaviour. There is an instant of confusion, perhaps a little cringe or shudder, and then an acceptance mixed with a strong desire to do better.

It is only now that you are ready to go forward. Only now are you able to shake yourself awake, walk away from that tempting restful sleepiness by the open window. And most importantly, you are now ready to go before the Council.

The Council
Most of the world's ancient religions and beliefs share the idea of a judgement that waits for us all when we die. In some of those traditions, the judgement is dramatic and immediate: we die, are judged, and at once are either elevated to heaven or paradise, or flung into the pit of hell. The decision made about the soul in these cases seems to have been made before the person's death, and we seem to have almost no say in the matter of which direction we go in!

But judgement in these cases is too easy a fate. It removes all the responsibility of the soul and, more importantly, ends the soul's journey: up or down, heaven or hell, end of story. God has spoken, say the traditional religions, and that's that.

When is life ever this simplistic? When do complicated actions ever elicit clear, dramatic results? Surely, if every action has an equal and opposite reaction, the incredibly complicated series of actions that make up a human life require an equally complex, sophisticated series of reactions?

Which is why the Council, in my experience, does not sit in

45

judgement. Certainly it is a terribly stern and imperious group of souls whom you face: we interpret them as people, perhaps ten men and women sitting at a huge table, or ten elders arranged around a kraal, and they are clearly not souls to be trifled with. They are immediately recognizable as hugely experienced, and possess a gravity and dignity that makes the whole experience very daunting.

The councillors are not archangels, or even angels. They are not fragments of God, or not at least any more than any of us are fragments of God. They are not all-powerful. In fact they have to answer to angels who supervise their efforts. I hate to use a comparison from the business world, which is about as far from God and spiritual enlightenment as you can get, but councillors are middle management. Except they don't have reserved parking and they actually have to come to work ...

Like any good committee of trusted lieutenants, the Council is appointed from a much higher level. Just as in the corporate world it is too much to hope that The Boss actually stubs out his cigar and makes the call himself, so the appointments are made by beings on much higher levels, but beings nonetheless still some way from their final reunion with God, when they all become partners in the greatest firm of all.

Kabbalistic writings speak of a fourth heaven; one where our concrete realities have long since become irrelevant and given way to a far more accurate perception of the light and heat of God's energies. And this is where our human imagination rolls over and gives up. Some histories of Australia suggest that when the European colonists first arrived in their ships, the aboriginal inhabitants literally failed to see them coming. Their eyes were directed at the masts and sails, at the huge wooden structures, at the white men in red clothes, but they registered nothing but the sea and gulls and sky. The reason suggested for this apparent blindness is that the ships and white men were like nothing the aborigines had ever encountered. They were a totally alien concept, and seemed to suggest that we as humans cannot physically see what we can't imagine. In your mind picture a kettle. Now picture a tube of toothpaste. Now imagine a tygorthrope. Not so easy, is it? Tygorthropes don't exist, and so you can't picture one in your head. We often say, 'I can't imagine what it would have been like,' or 'I can't imagine why he said that,' but of course this isn't strictly true: we always have a variety of possible answers to those questions in our imaginations. In other words, imagination is tricky: if you can imagine something, you will. If you can't, you won't. You can't imagine something you can't imagine.

So when I say that we can't possibly imagine what the fourth heaven is like, I'm not saying it only for effect. Perhaps you're imagining a universe of light. Wrong. It's not light. Dark? No. Space? No. Pink polka dots? No. Stop trying, because you simply can't. You're not able to, not now, and not for a very long time.

I know abstraction is frustrating. We want pictures, senses. But just for now try to do without thinking of a concrete image for the fourth heaven. As God said to Moses from the burning bush, I am what I am. The fourth heaven is what it is. But a more concrete creation is found here, according to Kabbalah.

You and I know that humans are imperfect. We're all flawed. We can be imperfect mentally, emotionally, spiritually, physically. A staggeringly beautiful athlete, with perfect hair and perfect proportions and flawless skin, can be as thick as a plank and emotionally abusive. A saint, dealing out kindness and selflessness and comfort, can be bent double with arthritis. As for intellectual perfection, well, this seems literally impossible: we simply cannot know everything there is to be known in our own little towns and countries, let alone our world.

So why make humans at all? If you were a scientist in a laboratory, with all the ingredients you needed to make life, why would you start on a project that was doomed to imperfection?

Surely you'd rather make yourself a little Frankenstein version of a cockroach or an orchid, or any one of the multitude of living things that seem to work so beautifully, so perfectly?

But just because you've never seen an example of a perfect human being, does it mean a perfect human being cannot ever be possible? You've never drawn a perfect circle (mine always end up looking a bit eggish!) but you still believe that perfect circles exist. Unless you have a terribly romantic spouse, or have been very lucky, you've probably never had an absolutely perfect evening, and yet you can easily imagine what it would be like, right down to the smallest details.

In the same way, God has a perfect idea of us as human beings. Christians believe that He created us in His image, and that's got to count for something. Perhaps we've fallen from grace, forgotten our heavenly roots and spiritual duties, but we're still based on a perfect original idea.

And the embodiment of that perfect original idea is known by Kabbalah as the Messiah. Christians will know this being as Jesus Christ; Jews still await His (or Her!) arrival. The Messiah is not of flesh and blood, because real flesh and real blood age and die. It is a manifestation, almost an abstract idea given life.

But the Messiah is not alone in the fourth heaven, named Zvul by Kabbalistic sages and sometimes known as the level of habitation. At his feet (I say 'his' for convenience, but all beings beyond our own world, even those in the first level of the Hereafter, are sexless) sit ten great spiritual masters. These are souls far advanced on their journey, possessing wisdom and knowledge that are, once again, far beyond the little limits of our mortal imagination. They are not angelic, and they are not the saints spoken of by various religions. There are more creations in the universe than we have the faintest idea of: God has made many many souls, and many beings. I feel that they were originally human men and women, who have perfected themselves to such a degree that they are permitted to accompany the absolutely perfect human. Because they were humans they are not perfect themselves, and will never be perfect; but they have reached the ultimate stage of development as human souls. What awaits them further – the unimaginable heavens closer to the final reunion with God – is a mystery.

Perhaps it's important here to explain something. Great enlightenment doesn't equal great power. And the most obvious example of this is that those almost perfect heavenly councillors, the companions of the Messiah, can't move to lower levels. You might think that such awesome souls could do more or less whatever they wanted, either in our world or the next four that await us, but this is not the case. I've explained how these levels lie on different frequencies or vibrational planes, and it's this that blocks them. Their frequency is so high, so elevated in the universe, that they literally cannot go any lower.

Yes, they guide all of us in our slow evolution, but they do it from a very great distance, metaphorically speaking. If the Council is middle management, these ten great councillors are the Board of Directors!

But this brief crash-course in Kabbalistic theology can no longer delay the inevitable Interview that was awaiting us some pages earlier! Where were we? Ah, yes: we were facing the Council. We were sweating a little. We were feeling very small.

And with good reason. Each one of us must face the Council after we've reviewed the life that has just passed. It is an interrogation, a ferocious cross-examination, and even though the Council itself is a projection or manifestation designed to appear familiar to us, it is by far the most intimidating and exposing experience we will ever have, in this life or the next. There is nothing blissful about this group. They are not a choir of angels. If a child has broken something, it's not going to be praised. And we've been breaking things like bulls in china shops.

49

But children always get a second chance to do the right thing, to undo some of the damage they have caused, and the Council operates in a similar way. However, you are no longer bound by your earthly age: we are all 'adults' in the Hereafter, able to make decisions and able to understand responsibilities and consequences, and there is no soft-soaping or euphemism in the way the Council interrogates us.

So are we being cross-examined in order to get us to slip up? Is this some sort of elaborate way to get us to confess to sins? Not at all. The role of the Council is to pick at every aspect of our past lives, not so that they can find fault or condemn us, but so that we can assess ourselves more accurately. Because only through assessing ourselves completely and honestly can we discover what we need to change about ourselves. Psychologists in this world provide a similar service, albeit in far more reassuring circumstances! They ask endless questions, pick and probe and question. Often they ask us questions we can't answer, and as soon as that happens we know we have to go deeper, question more intensely.

Perhaps the Council is stern and intimidating, to ensure that we are honest in our evaluation. Perhaps it is to underline that self-knowledge is not something to be taken lightly or dealt with in half-measures. Whatever the answer, the Council invariably succeeds in untangling the knotted strings of ego and delusion. Our pretensions and assumptions about ourselves are stripped away to nothing, and finally we are ready to embark on our new life. And it is here that the Council gives us a choice, an enormous and wonderful choice: *Either you stay, or you go.* Stay, and learn as much as you can. Experience the vast resources of knowledge and wisdom available in the first level, and come closer to understanding your soul and its place in God's universe.

Go, and reincarnate on earth. Learn and grow by experience, by being born and living and bleeding and loving, and making horrible mistakes, and achieving great triumphs.

Pondering the immensity of this choice, and the infinitely marvellous implications of both choices, the soul can finally wander back to those living people it has left behind. It is now accepting of its new state, and enormously energized by what it has just seen and heard; and for the first time the pleasures of our earthly world and the bonds of human love seem somewhat dimmed.

Nevertheless, now is the time to contact our earthly family, for whatever reason we might want to do that. Some spirits I've encountered go to their funeral, and watch with an amused or interested eye to see who is there and who isn't. I sometimes get dead people coming to me and asking me if I'll tell their family that they really liked the funeral; that the flowers were lovely and the speeches were really good, but they don't want their ashes stored on the mantelpiece or scattered in this or that place. The spirits of those who love us are never gone for good, but this moment is when they finally detach themselves entirely from our world and our life, and stop wanting their old lives back.

So what will it be? If you were given the choice today, what would you do? Stay or go? Learn or live? It would seem that the journey is about to get interesting.

For some, at least.

For others it's about to get ugly …

3

Damnation!

Is there a hell?

Five minutes into the movie *Kindergarten Cop*, Arnold Schwarzenegger has blasted his way into a den of vice, a sort of night-club version of Sodom and Gomorrah, and is standing over the debris with a still-smoking cannon, buzz-cut bristling and jaw-muscles rippling.

'Who are you?' asks one terrified lowlife, picking shrapnel out of his shoulder-pads and gelled hair (this was the early 1990s, remember).

Arnie fixes him with a beady Teutonic eye: 'I'm da party-pooper!'

Well I'm afraid it's time for me to poop da party. So far it's mostly been happiness and forgiveness, therapy for confused souls, the vast compassion of God, and the good news about the survivability of death; but there's no such thing as a free lunch, either in this world or those that follow. It's time to recognize that hell exists. People go to hell. Bad people go to hell. Good people go to hell.

Have you noticed how nobody seems to want to have a good

old-fashioned conversation or debate on good old-fashioned issues of damnation and fire and brimstone any more? Have you noticed how the whole concept of a bad afterlife seems to have become the preserve of fundamentalists and conservative fruit-cakes?

The fact is that the idea of purgatory, or some kind of punishment after we die, has become very unfashionable over the last generation or two. Just think how Hollywood portrays people who believe in an otherworldly punishment: crazy old hillbillies doused in moonshine, shifty-eyed voodoo priestesses living in a swamp, vengeance-obsessed suicide bombers frothing over their beards ...

Why has this shift happened? Why have ordinary people, many of whom believe in God and badly want to believe in some sort of heavenly reward, rejected with contempt the idea of hell or purgatory?

Perhaps an obvious answer is the role in our society of academics and professional intellectuals, who have increasingly managed to get their faces into the public eye. This group (which all too often pay their bills at the expense of moral beliefs) have seized the higher ground, insisting that anyone who believes in either heaven or hell is deluding themselves. How, they ask, can we still entertain these Medieval ideas? Surely we've come to understand over the last 2000 years that all religions are parables, that God is merely a creation of our species, something to give us hope? As for hell – let's just say if you want to ruin a dinner party hosted by an atheist, try expressing a belief that hell exists!

Because of course these thinkers, whose vanity has led them to believe that humans are the creators (and that they, as intellectuals, are at the top of that elite human pile!), will tell you that hell is just another idea invented by our clever little minds. Oh yes, hell exists, they say, but it exists in this world, this tangible world, the only world that exists. What could be worse, they ask, than the gore and darkness and emotional numbness and pointlessness of hand-to-hand combat? How could hell be worse than the dankest dungeon in a slave-barracks? Who needs imaginary torments when poverty, disease and environmental degradation stalk our world?

But the main reason nobody talks about spiritual punishment is simple: if you don't believe in sin, you can't believe in punishment.

The rehabilitation of sin

Once upon a time people knew where they stood. If you did x, y would happen. Whether these guidelines came from religious laws or civil society, or were unspoken but just understood by the general community, they kept people in relative peace and order. Most of these rules or guidelines quickly became moral pronouncements. After all, rules are enforced in only two ways: either somebody uses force on you, or you understand their value and so obey them.

We feel that it is simply wrong to kill someone. We instinctively understand the huge moral condemnation that would go with such an action, and we shudder at the thought of crossing that line. Darwinists will tell you that such self-discipline is a natural instinct: if we killed each other whenever we felt like it, we'd be a pitiful little species!

But whether it's nature or nurture, our entire society is governed by a huge web of laws and moral restrictions. For thousands of years people believed that to break those laws was to sin. And to sin was the worst act imaginable, a direct attack on God and the integrity of your soul.

But what happens when your belief in God starts wavering? What happens when you start thinking of religion in terms of mere symbol or allegory; when God fades from being a huge, demanding force in the universe to being a friendly suburban feel-good 'inspiration'; when you no longer need to worship in a church or cathedral or on a mountaintop, but can say conceited little prayers in your garden at home?

The result is obvious: lose sight of God's immensity, and the demands of pushing your soul towards learning and growth, and you lose sight of sin and evil. In short, we've been acting like children. We've convinced ourselves of an almost real (but still very vague), pleasant afterlife, and completely denied the possibility of a sinister one.

Perhaps I'm being too puritanical by mentioning the Ten Commandments of Moses and the Seven Deadly Sins of the Catholic Church, but as a moral blueprint they seem to have worked slightly better than, say, the Atkins Diet. And more importantly they offer us a fascinating – and to my mind chilling – insight into how our modern world is actively encouraging us to break the moral and practical laws that have served our species well enough for millennia.

Let's start with the Ten Commandments:

1. Thou shalt not kill.
   Okay, we won't. But we'll call for our government to kill criminals, and we'll vote for presidents who wage wars, and we'll pay thirty bucks to watch people kill each other at the movies.

2. Thou shalt not commit adultery.
   If 30% of spouses are having affairs, can it be so wrong? After all, every magazine and television show tells us to follow our hearts …

3. Thou shalt not steal.
   Except from the government, in the form of tax evasion, right? And what's the harm in nicking the odd pack of smokes?

4. Thou shalt not bear false witness against they neighbour.
   Unless he's a Jew or black or a Rastafarian, or you don't like the way his dog barks all night, or you suspect he's stealing your newspaper. Or, like the citizens of the oh-so-holy Salem, the neighbours who won't sell you their ground suddenly and conveniently start worshipping Satan.

5. Thou shalt not covet anything that is thy neighbour's.
   Odd, then, that we should be told every night by advertisers on television to want what our neighbours have: beautiful wives, beautiful children, a big car, a big house …

6. Thou shalt have no other god before me.
   Well, you see, we understand today that the Bible was far too literal. So it's fine for us to worship whatever god we feel we like. Like money, for example: that's fun to worship.

7. Thou shalt not make unto thee any graven image.
   Okay, this one might be a little archaic as laws go. Or at least let's hope it's not strictly enforced in the Hereafter for the sake of our daughters: buy her Barbie, damn her to hell? I hope not.

8. Thou shalt not take the name of the Lord thy God in vain.
   Jesus Christ! What are we supposed to say when we're frustrated? I mean, God!

9. Remember the Sabbath day, to keep it holy.
   Sabbath? Is that Friday, when we go and get plastered, or Sunday, when we yell abuse at footballers on the telly?

10. Honour thy father and mother.
    Okay, what better way to honour them than by sticking them in a state-run home and visiting them once a month?

And then of course there are the Seven Deadly Sins. Let's face it: they've become the Seven Holy Laws of Marketing.

Pride: having great self-esteem, so that you can live life to the fullest and have everything you deserve (which is everything!). The virtue from which all others arise – Oprah and Dr Phil would no doubt agree. Vanity is just a reflection of good self-esteem, not so?

Envy: you need to be as good as everyone else, which means you need to buy everything they have. Envy is a natural emotion, merely an instinct that helps you to keep up with the pack.

Gluttony: make every day a McDonald's day! If you're fat, it's probably a metabolic problem.

Lust: the more people you sleep with, and the less you care about each of them, the more sophisticated you are. *Sex and the City* and *Cosmopolitan* say so, so it must be true.

Anger: don't get mad, get even. Buy a Volkswagen.

Greed: having beautiful things is a reflection of a beautiful soul. A popular church in South Africa even teaches its followers that God wants us to make lots of money, because the more money we have the more money He has. Wait, that's not it …

Sloth: chill out, relax – you deserve the rest. Come on, put your feet up. Watch TV for five hours a day.

What with this constant barrage of reassurance, this continuous denial of the existence of sin, it's no wonder that we are picking and choosing our morals more than ever. And we've all figured out our own little reasons and theological arguments to defend our beliefs: killing is bad because, well, er, it just is, but being promiscuous is fine because it's done with free will and doesn't hurt anyone else. White lies, little fibs, harmless fantasies, cruel things said 'in jest': the lines blur further with every year that passes.

And then one day we die. And it all gets very real, very quickly. Oops.

The Grey Zones

This is where I stop talking about hell. Hell is an old idea, filled with infamous images of pitchforks and fire. Hell changes, too, from culture to culture, appearing as the worst thing a particular society could imagine. To the Inuit and the Vikings, hell was a frozen wasteland; flames and red-hot pokers would have seemed heavenly! To Christians and Muslims, living in the baking deserts of the Middle East, hellish torment could only be heat and everlasting fire.

But there is a world, a zone, that exists to confront and purge evil. The Universe is not a massage course or a self-esteem booster: there are dark forces in it, and people (as we know all too well) do terrible things to themselves and each other, and these people cannot be given a hug and told that everything is all right. These people enter the Grey Zones, the dark slumlands of purgatory.

Here there are no pitchforks and fire, no smouldering caves or icy wastes. There is nothing at all, except a timeless spiritual numbness. This is a grey world of immense loneliness and disorientation, and the hopeless misery experienced here is of a kind we cannot easily imagine. The soul fallen into this world is surrounded by millions of others just like itself, but it cannot feel them or see them.

There are no macabre thrills for the onlooker in the Grey Zones. There is no sadistic torture by demons, no superficial pyrotechnics. It is a more disturbing horror. I've seen this place and the deadness that saturates every soul, every dull, hazy moment of this place, is truly horrible.

In my analogy of the Apollo rocket blasting off, I spoke of the astral body that we all have, that it is an intangible in this world but nonetheless quite 'concrete' by the standards of the Hereafter. I said that ghosts are manifestations of that astral body, when souls are unwilling or unable to leave this world for the next, and become stuck. The astral is a plane closely bound with earthly desire and a failure to look beyond the literal and the temporary. It is a slow, dark vibration, something like being drunk but without the general feeling of well-being. And it is on this 'level' or frequency or vibration that the Grey Zones exist.

Traditional takes on hell or the realm of punishment that awaits sinners are that these unfortunate souls are literally flung down into the pit by God or the angels; that at the moment of death they fall, in a quite physical way, down into whatever ghastly fate awaits them. In the film *Angel Heart*, when Mickey Rourke's character ends up taking a rickety lift down a long dark shaft, we know where he's going (you don't mess with a demonic Robert de Niro and walk away!), and he is clearly trapped.

In all these cases the souls heading on down to the basement of the universe definitely don't want to be going there. They fall screaming, or claw and cling and beg for forgiveness, or, in the case of the film, try to fight against the terror they feel closing in on them.

But the reality of the Grey Zones is quite different, and people struggle to understand this when I explain it to them. Because souls aren't flung into slumlands. They are drawn to them. They are attracted to the Grey Zones.

Why on earth would anyone be attracted to this place, you might ask? It just doesn't make any sense. But it is important to understand that attraction has nothing to do with common sense or morality. A syringe full of heroin exerts an overwhelming pull on an addict. The married man who cannot keep his hands off his flirtatious secretary is giving in to an attraction that defies logic or morality. On a far more everyday level, have you ever had the experience of getting up, going to your car and driving to the shop just to buy a chocolate? That chocolate was pulling you, compelling you to come and get it, and despite being an extraordinary creation with an amazing brain and God-given free will, you jumped into your car and obeyed the call of a tiny lump of sugar!

Those who once would have been called sinners, and today are called social misfits or criminals, are compelled to act in certain ways on earth. The killer may feel terrible remorse, but can't understand how he did what he did. Many murderers or rapists talk as if they were forced by something not in themselves to commit their crimes: I don't know what I was thinking; I was out of my mind; the devil made me do it. In short, these people have no self-awareness, no understanding of their own dark currents, which means they have no insight into spiritual matters and are horribly detached from their souls.

And it is exactly this lack of self-awareness, and particularly the obsession with worldly matters, that attracts the soul to the astral level. People who have committed terrible crimes in this world almost invariably are those who are selfish, ignorant and spiritually numb. Without knowing it, they are perfect fodder for the astral, and when they die their transition to that realm is a foregone conclusion.

But not only murderers and rapists go to the Grey Zones. Any obsession with material things in the world indicates someone badly out of touch with the realities of the universe. There are many addictions in our world – sex, drugs, money, power – and all numb the soul further and drive a greater wedge between it and God. Even those who lived relatively good lives, but refused to accept even the possibility of life after death and crossed over raging and fighting (in other words, desperately trying to cling on to earthly life), find themselves in the slumlands.

Of course there are always difficult cases when considering who is likely to face punishment and who isn't. For example, can soldiers be considered murderers? Is it worse for a soldier to kill an unarmed woman or child than it is for him to kill another soldier? Can a soldier be held responsible by the universe or God if he didn't understand what he was doing? What about the Nazis who were 'only following orders'?

These are difficult questions, but all must bow to a very straightforward and unchanging reality: any person who kills another person, regardless of the circumstances, has burdened their soul with negative karma, and will face some sort of reckoning. But as in the case of abortion, there seems to a sliding scale. Soldiers who are brainwashed or deeply traumatized by previous encounters with violence and death seem to attract a less terrible karma that those who enjoy the killing, or those who kill with a clear understanding of what they are doing. For instance, the Nazi officer Adolf Eichmann, who supervised the killing of millions of Jews in the Second World War, was questioned on exactly this point: did he understand the difference between right and wrong? His answers revealed him to be an educated man, with a solid knowledge of various philosophies, including classical definitions of right and wrong. One might argue that someone capable of doing what Eichmann did cannot possibly understand the difference between right and wrong, that he must have been psychotic or mad. But the human soul is capable of greatness, bc it great good or great evil, and evil doesn't always have to involve demonic cackling and devilish plans to take over the world. It can merely present as an entirely numb, terribly efficient man like Eichmann.

Manifesting ugliness

I've explained how souls who pass over to what we call the first level of heaven see and experience only what they can deal with, and what they expect. In other words, they are manifesting a new reality for themselves simply from their own thoughts and expectations.

This kind of manifestation works in exactly the same way in the Grey Zones. But hold the phone, you're saying: why then don't souls just manifest themselves a comfortable yacht and some cold beers, or manifest themselves straight into heaven?

A fair question, until you start to think about practical examples, in this world. How often don't we hear from murder trials that the killer was molested as a child, or suffered from depression, or believed he was possessed by demons? How often aren't rapists themselves victims of childhood sexual and physical abuse? In other words, these people's minds are filled only with fear and pain and rage and cruelty. How can such a mind, such a vandalized soul, manifest anything but squalor and confusion?

Here's another example, based on the sort of soul that will, in my experience, find itself in a very bad place straight after death. Mrs Smith, beautiful and vacuous, has been raised to believe that she is the most exquisite creature in the world and deserves everything she wants. Since the age of thirteen she has dedicated almost every waking hour to looking gorgeous. For a while she hunted husbands, eventually picking one rich enough to subsidize her lifestyle and good-looking enough to guarantee her beautiful children. The birth of a daughter enabled Mrs Smith to start teaching the child everything she knows. Which is nothing.

Yes, Mrs Smith gives to charity, and yes, she's never hurt anyone (deliberately). But she cannot see that her whole life has focused on herself: what she wants, what she needs. It has been a life completely cut off from the realities of our world, and from the demands of the spirit. When she gets depressed, she takes pills rather than finding out why she feels this way. When she thinks about death, she has another face-lift to feel younger, rather than facing the huge questions and understanding the wonderful processes and stages of life and death.

In short, Mrs Smith's soul is empty, but more than that it is ugly, mutated and twisted by the petty little desires of this world. And when Mrs Smith dies and finds herself in the dark, empty wastes, she will be hideously ugly. Of course she will try to manifest the kind of the beauty she knew in this life, but this means nothing in the Hereafter. Being an ugly person has nothing to do with how smooth your skin is or how pretty your eyes are. Of course the astral, being a particularly vicious place, will enable Mrs Smith to manifest some limited accessories: her attempts to dress herself in furs will leave her wearing a sack.

And this is the torment we find in the Grey Zones. Not devils with hot pokers, but our worst fears about ourselves. Souls who crossed over bitter or twisted have no one to project all that poison at, and so torture themselves. Murderers, crossing over with guilt and fear and loathing, suddenly find themselves at the receiving end of their own evils.

Of the greatest punishments that await all souls in the slumlands are loneliness and confusion. Human beings can bear almost any suffering, be it torture or grief or madness, as long as they are near other people, and have some scrap of order or control over their lives. In his book *Nam*, Mark Baker describes how one American captured by the Viet Cong was locked up by himself for years. Suicide was impossible, and so to prevent himself from losing his mind this prisoner built his dream house in his head. Imagining, in real time, levelling the foundations, mixing the cement, and so on, saved him: whole afternoons would go by as he imagined mowing the lawn, a foot at a time. Take away that blessed human gift of imagination, and the prisoner would not have been able to impose any structure on his solitude. Likewise, many prisoners of war find themselves creating patterns and routines out of anything: the changing of the guard, a daily truck delivering supplies. Anything to keep in touch with order and reality.

The souls in the Grey Zones are not so lucky. They are unable to find order in anything, unable to impose routines on their time, because there is no time, no set patterns. They are entirely focused on their own torments, and so are blind to those around them; and this perceived solitude simply magnifies their agonies. It is a vicious circle of suffering. At least if you get poked in the bum with a fork, you can scream or curse the devil or hate Satan. There is some power and relief in reacting like this. But when you are your own jailer and torturer, there is no relief.

What about people whose crimes were so monstrous, and whose actions destroyed the lives of so many people, that even such self-torment seems too lenient? What about Eichmann? What about the hit-squads of all the miserable, sordid little wars and revolutions of the 20th century? What about all those who killed mercilessly, and enjoyed it?

God is compassionate. God is endlessly merciful. But God is also just, and His creation demands justice. More than that, He demands that we learn, and learning can often only happen through suffering. The punishment for people who have committed crimes against humanity is truly terrible, and perhaps more than we in this life can imagine. Because, in a single instant, with a sickening, world-imploding, heart-destroying impact, the perpetrators of these crimes take on all the anguish and sorrow of their victims. And then, like a great wave of death and pain, they feel also the grief and agony of the families, the lovers, the husbands and wives, the children, of all those they killed. A living human being in our world would certainly die at once if exposed to this kind of emotional and psychological onslaught: our minds would snap, our bodies surrender at once. But the condemned soul of the perpetrator has no such escape into death and forgetfulness. They must feel every twist of a million knives, endure every broken heart.

And what of those who sit safe and unbloodied in their offices, far away from the fighting, but who have given the order that sent thousands of men to their deaths, or condemned tens of thousands of civilians to be burned and bombed? What of those who ordered for Guernica, Coventry, London, Paris to be bombed? Or of those who, in what we call 'legitimate' retaliation, ordered Berlin and Dresden to be flattened? Hiroshima?

Those who plan and feed wars, whether on the offensive or defensive side, will suffer terribly. It seems unfair that a defensive act should be condemned. But killing is killing, whatever its justification. Did Gandhi shoot back? American president Harry Truman did shoot back, in a terrible way. In 1945 he became the first, and thank God the only, president to authorize the dropping of a nuclear bomb on civilian targets, the doomed Hiroshima and Nagasaki.

Military historians still argue about whether it was right or wrong in terms of ending the war quickly, but the fact remains that Truman decided, rationally and with full knowledge of the consequences, to kill 100,000 people in a single stroke.

Truman's punishment has come and gone now, but I can't begin to imagine it: every one of those Japanese souls writhing in agony and terror, exploding into his consciousness in a single scream as he died and faced the spiritual consequences of his actions. No soul, however calm and prepared for death, can survive such a hellish experience unaltered. Truman was tortured because of his decision. Truman has seen hell, in whichever form you can imagine it.

Does this seem too harsh? After all, historians will tell you that Truman's decision was a horrible one to have to make: either drop the bombs or have the war go on for months, possibly with tens of thousands of more American deaths as the Japanese fought to the last on their home soil. Other historians will tell you that Japan was about to crumble anyway, and that the war would have been over in weeks without having to drop the bombs.

But at the time it must have seemed a no-win choice: damned if he did and damned if he didn't. And this is one of the most awful things about war. It forces people into a position where killing is the only option. It is how we deal with that nightmarish world that elevates or condemns us. Truman's position was particularly horrible: ordering deaths with a clear head – and above all, a sharp and well-developed mind – carries a terrible karmic penalty. Turning our greatest gift from God, our intelligence, to killing is an obscenity.

So can we judge Truman? Was his punishment just? Frankly, that's none of our business. Sure, we can judge, but it means nothing. Only God can judge, and God has judged. The price is paid. Those who want power, especially the power to destroy nations by unleashing nuclear weapons on them, either have to understand their spiritual responsibilities, or be taught them.

My sense is that Truman survived his hellish torture. Many lesser souls would have collapsed into an endless cycle of despair and hatred of themselves and of the universe, but Truman eventually raised his head and saw the possibility of redemption. He is alive today, reincarnated into one of the families his decision shattered. He is of low birth, living a relatively hard life in Japan, and he's come back with a mark on his back, a birthmark that looks like a burn. I know almost nothing about his life as President Truman, and don't know if he had a birthmark then, but now he is most definitely marked.

Redemption

The Grey Zones: dim and slow, muddy slumlands where the spark of life is extinguished, where hope is unimaginable. Souls wander, bound up tightly in their own overwhelming disgust, besieged by fear and confusion. They are surrounded by shuffling shapes, but entirely alone. They gnaw constantly on the knots of their mental prison, but are unable to think.

And then they look up.

Have you ever been consumed by grief or fear or anger, when the world seems to crumple into a small, constricting cage? Even your breathing is shallow. Your sleep is restless and filled with feverish dreams, or you sleep for too long and wake exhausted. The world beyond your life seems so terribly dim, so far away.

Many people live in this world, walking among us, their eyes cast down as they fight to survive against the dark pull of mental illness or addiction. But many of these people reach a point of realization: this is no way to live. Suddenly, like a beam of light blazing through the slats of a shutter, they realize that they are alone and wretched. Drug addicts and alcoholics talk about a 'moment of clarity'. Whether it hits them like a bolt from the blue, or whether they have arrived at that point through years of counselling or therapy, it is a profound experience, and one that often leads to salvation.

But such realizations aren't limited to our mortal world.

Sometimes it happens that a soul in the Grey Zones will stop, and almost stumble for a moment. He stares ahead at the dim, hazy ground before him. A sound – a sense. No, he thinks, it is nothing, there is nothing here except the horrifying flatness of grief and suffering stretched thin. And then suddenly it comes again. There is something else. Someone else. In the darkness beyond. A figure, no longer just a tormenting reflection of his own misery or the souls of those he caused to suffer. Another figure, a stranger, bringing mystery and wonder, and – he can hardly dare to think it – hope.

And so two souls meet, or a solitary soul suddenly remembers the existence of others. And at this moment he knows something concrete for the first time in aeons: I don't want to be here any more.

It is a flash of insight that seems fairly obvious to you or me in this world, but it is a remarkable and profound one for the soul in the Grey Zones. It marks the beginning of redemption, and is the moment in which the soul has started moving forward once again.

But we can't do it alone. In our everyday world we've met or read about counsellors, teachers, role-models, in short a host of benevolent spirits who have dedicated their lives to pulling people out of the pit of despair or addiction or violence. And the same hope is always offered to those trapped in the gloom of the astral. There are beings, which to keep it simple I'll call angels, who can reach down into the darkness towards these souls just starting to realize their pitiful state. Many souls can't be reached: after all, you can't be helped if you don't accept that there is a problem. If you're looking at the ground, you can't see the stars. But for those who have made that apparently obvious connection – that purgatory sucks! – these helpers provide a brief glimpse of higher possibilities, and the real potential for redemption.

It is often only a glimpse: the vibrations of the Grey Zones are low and dark, and the angelic life-savers can't exist or operate on such low levels. They simply can't – and simply won't – taint their beautiful selves with the squalor of the lower frequencies. And so they need the soul in question to reach up to them, to take the first step on their own, without any prompting or help. They are not hovering in the sky over the slumlands, plucking souls out of the mud with loud slurping sounds! They're not the Marines rescuing people off embassy roofs. They help only those who want to be helped, and who are ready to be helped.

Of course this raises a fascinating question about the experiences of those souls who don't believe in redemption, or believe in eternal damnation. If this realm is a projection like the higher first level of heaven, then surely we make of it what we expect? And if a fundamentalist Christian or Muslim believes in a never-ending torment of fire and persecution, how are they going to be in any condition to look up to the light?

Perhaps you could even go so far as to suggest that some people don't ever want to be saved. You might have met people like this already: people who take a sick and hollow pleasure in being miserable and imposing all kinds of suffering on themselves. Medieval monks, believing that they were dastardly sinners, flogged themselves in an orgy of self-hatred and self-righteousness. Of course this was a petty and essentially lazy response to life. Isn't it much easier to punish yourself for the past than it is to act decisively for a better future? Those who wring their hands and despise themselves for imagined sins are copping out of life. Their journey has stalled, and they are indulging themselves rather than moving on and moving up.

It is these people who expect the worst because secretly they want the worst. And they want the worst because the worst does not require you to grow. It only requires you to endure, to cope, to survive. The only thing the worst teaches us about is our darkness and our endurance. It doesn't teach us how to live, or how to be free, or how to strive or endeavour.

At times I've been harangued by devout Catholics who tell me that I'm also a Catholic because they think my beliefs – and specifically my beliefs about the Grey Zones – are in accordance with the basic foundations of Catholicism. Of course, they then read more about my work or they come to a session, and generally come to the conclusion that I'm a devil-worshipper or witch. Suddenly, enthusiastic inquisitors become a little Spanish for my liking. It's funny, but only up to a point.

But I certainly agree with Catholicism in one respect. I've seen what a difference it can make to pray for souls in purgatory. Not to pray for their pain or suffering to be less; they are there to learn, and there to rid their souls of the sordidness that got them there in the first place. But to pray for the moment that they realize they want more, they want something better.

Suicide and damnation

The Catholic Church has always been clear about what awaits those who commit suicide: if you commit murder, you have committed a mortal, damnable sin, and suicide is nothing more than self-murder. Take your own life as a Catholic, and eternal hellfire awaits. Perhaps we can gain some sobering insight into the depths the human soul can fall, when we realize that the devout Catholics who choose to kill themselves are certain they're going to an eternity of horror, but do it anyway. Perhaps there are torments that the human soul is literally unable to deal with.

The reality of suicide is more complex than clear black-and-white moral judgements, but what is certain is that those who do kill themselves will go to the slumlands. This is not a punishment from God, but a reflection of the terrible numbness and confusion of their souls. Remember, we usually get what we expect to get, and those who are desperate and unhinged enough to kill themselves probably weren't realistically expecting anything more than an escape from their reality, which is of course a terribly limited mindset, and one that automatically excludes them from any higher spiritual vibrations.

I've been approached by people wanting to take their own lives, and wanting some reassurance from me as to where they're going. Without really knowing it themselves, they want me to give them a push off that ledge, but what I tell them is always a disappointment.

Most of them come with the idea that if they're self-aware, in other words have made peace with their motive and have taken responsibility for their action, they'll be self-aware on the other side, or at least go to a place that rewards them for their insight. Of course they've failed to understand that no suicide can ever be committed 'responsibly', in terms of the suffering it causes those who have been left behind; that self-murder is often the most selfish and destructive act a human can commit.

But most importantly, self-awareness in this life (even the limited and mangled self-awareness of those who commit suicide) counts for nothing once they have entered the Grey Zones. Like all those lost and lonely souls in that purgatorial realm, they will be in a state of absolute confusion, and will remember nothing of what they knew in this life.

There is, however, a single exception to all of this. People suffering with terrible illnesses, either physical or mental, who choose to commit suicide do not go to the Grey Zones. Like any sufferer of a traumatic death they pass through into the first level and are slowly calmed and made aware of their new state. Choosing euthanasia or assisted suicide for these people is not enough to take them to the Grey Zones. However, those administering the euthanasia should know that with any action there is a karmic price attached: easing the suffering of a dying or suffering person by administering euthanasia is vastly different to committing bloody murder, but nevertheless one is taking a life and there will be consequences.

Each action has an equal and opposite reaction. No matter what the circumstances, suicide is self-murder, and there will be a price to pay. But always remember this: God is merciful. God doesn't hold grudges. And God never forgets us, never leaves us to rot. *Redemption is always waiting. Ascension is always waiting.*

A person who has committed suicide is just as likely as any other suffering soul to look up and see the angelic helpers. Purged of their sin, their karmic penalty largely paid, and armed with that soul-transforming resolve to find a better path, there is every chance that they will shake off their dark burden and move into the light and life and freedom of the Hereafter. There is always hope. Always.

Reincarnation

Little boy lost

James Leininger was born in the United States in 1998. His parents, Bruce and Andrea, are a conventional American middle-class modern couple: hardworking, sophisticated, comfortably off. Little James seemed to be heading for a totally normal childhood, of days in playschool and afternoons of chasing family pets or blowing away neighbourhood cars with imaginary ray-guns.

But very soon it became clear that James was not an ordinary child. Not yet two years old, he showed a fondness for toy aeroplanes that bordered on obsession. No other toys could hold his attention. And then in 2000 the nightmares started.

ABCNews.com, reporting the story in 2004, recounted how James' mother became deeply concerned by her two-year-old son's night-time terrors. 'I'd wake him up and he'd be screaming,' she said.

What had James been dreaming about? 'Airplane crash on fire, little man can't get out,' was his reply.

A year later James was as intent on aircraft as ever, and had begun to show an advanced knowledge of World War Two vintage aircraft, despite his family rarely watching television programmes or reading books on the subject. Toy planes would be thoroughly examined in what was clearly a kind of pre-flight check, and once when his mother pointed to what she called a bomb on the belly of one of the planes, James quickly corrected her, telling her it was a drop tank, a kind of fuel tank slung under the aircraft.

The Leiningers decided they needed a professional counsellor when James' nightmares worsened, and found one who was open to the idea of reincarnation. In these therapy sessions both parents and child began to consider the possibility that he was describing not dreams, but memories. And more importantly, memories that began to focus in on the life and death of a particular American fighter pilot.

At first the boy's uncannily detailed descriptions of aerial warfare described general topics, like the way the tyres of Corsair fighter planes in World War Two would take a pounding on landing. But soon he was telling his father about taking off from an aircraft carrier called *Natoma*, and mentioning someone called Jack Larson.

Then, said Bruce Leininger, James told him that he'd been shot down over the Pacific island of Iwo Jima. The child began to sign his drawings 'James 3'. Oh, and his aircraft had been brought down by a direct hit to its engine.

Frenzied research by Bruce revealed that the *Natoma* had been at Iwo Jima. Jack Larson was an elderly veteran living in Arkansas. And the only pilot from their squadron killed at Iwo Jima was one James M. Huston.

Finally, with evidence apparently too compelling to ignore, Bruce found a former aerial gunner who had seen Huston's aircraft destroyed.

'I would say he was hit head on,' the old man told ABC News, 'right in the middle of the engine.'

Today James' parents are convinced that he is the young pilot, 21-year-old Huston, reincarnated to work through the trauma of a violent, pointless death. Sceptics point out, perhaps rightly, that people are too eager to leap to paranormal conclusions – Professor Paul Kurtz of the State University of New York, included in the report, spoke of the Leiningers creating a 'fairy tale' – but in this case I entirely agree that little James is James Huston, killed on March 3, 1945.

A sensationalist example, to be sure, but I think it is a useful one. For many in the modern world the idea of reincarnation is unsettling, and is often dismissed as a flaky belief or an Eastern superstition, or else is condemned as a heresy that goes against the teachings of the Bible or Koran. Mention reincarnation to most sophisticated urban dwellers, and you get pitying looks. In fact they're fully expecting you to start eating lentil curry and hawking badly printed books on the power of crystals.

But what the Leiningers encountered would have seemed entirely natural to many in the East, where reincarnation is a commonly accepted phenomenon. From the Middle East across to China and Japan, many ancient beliefs and organized religions embrace the idea of returning souls, and many ordinary people live quite ordinary lives safe in the knowledge that they have been on earth before, and will be again.

Westerners have picked up an awful lot of rubbish from Oriental beliefs, and if you read this book you'll know that I am totally against the cultural and spiritual shopping around that many Westerners do, simply because they're too lazy or ignorant to explore their own cultures. Americans and Europeans have been played for suckers over and over in the last fifty years, embracing swamis or gurus who've milked them for money or publicity, or adopting rituals and diets simply because they're exotic and therefore somehow better than Western versions.

However, there is one aspect of Eastern spiritual awareness

that the West has overlooked to its detriment: that of reincarnation. Many Eastern beliefs are superstitions and no more mystical or profound than, say, not wanting to walk under a ladder; but reincarnation is not a superstition, nor a fashionable belief to be accepted or discarded lightly. It is an ancient reality in our human world, and one that you should try to separate from all the nonsense that has been written about it.

You'll have noticed so far that I'm really approaching this topic sideways, trying to ease you into it, simply because so many generalizations and inaccuracies have been written and spoken about it, and by so many desperately unbalanced or loony people.

Unfortunately these fruitcakes, harassing you on street-corners or demanding you buy their grubby little pamphlets, have prejudiced us against reincarnation. After all, who are you more likely to listen to: a Professor of Philosophy and Theology with a long white beard and twinkly eyes, or a shaved nutter in a sack who smells like last week's left-overs?

But even if you don't believe in reincarnation, or your religion doesn't allow you to, despite your curiosity about it, the chances are you already believe in limited reincarnation. Science calls it genetics, or genealogy, but if you've ever looked at a child and recognized his or her great-grandfather in an expression or a particular glance of the eyes, you've already acknowledged that some of our essence carries on through the generations and lives on long after we're dead.

It's important to be sceptical – or at least objective – about most things you hear, especially when it comes to Eastern mysticism. Remember, you're only hearing what people want you to hear, and if they're actively supplying you with information, it's probable they're being paid for their trouble. And if there's one thing you take away from this book, it's that money and faith can't and don't mix!

But I also believe that scepticism can get in the way of

spiritual realities. An example of this was evident in a recent television investigation into claims of reincarnation in India and Lebanon. In both cases, children between the ages of ten and fourteen had felt compelled to go to certain villages, where elderly couples immediately identified them as their own children who had died as babies or toddlers. While it is understandable for bereaved and lonely adults to want to believe something like this, it was in fact the children who supplied most of the information: how they'd died, who their siblings had been, what games they'd played. In a more intellectually cautious society like ours, the claims of both children and adults would have been ridiculed, or would have raised suspicions of trickery or fraud. In other words, this wonderful and ordained reunion would have been prevented from the outset, without any facts being investigated or claims tested.

Corrections

By now you know that reincarnation is a choice we make, after we've been questioned and guided by the Council. But what I didn't explain was just how clear that choice often is.

We all know that reflection without action is pointless. Why acknowledge past mistakes if you don't plan to do anything about them? You can just nod ruefully, and mess up all over again. Most religions remove this from the equation by making the Hereafter out to be a final destination: you get in or you don't, and if you do, there's nothing to reflect on, and no need to make any changes. A soul in heaven is hardly likely to want to improve itself, since God or St Peter or whoever let it through the Pearly Gates has already bestowed instant perfection on it.

But the Hereafter is a process, and a process means mistakes, and the chance to correct those mistakes. And this is where the soul standing before the Council is in for a shock. Yes, you've reviewed your past life in an astounding flash of consciousness, and yes, you've found three or four major flaws that you want to correct next time around. But wait a moment: haven't you been here before?

Of course you have! Reincarnation is a huge wheel, a cycle like the seasons that returns you to the Council again and again. Certainly it feels like your first time, but it isn't. Suddenly you've got that old sinking feeling of being caught in a lie you can't quite remember the details of. What did I tell them last time? What did I promise to fix, and what haven't I fixed?

I know it sounds somehow petty in comparison to the great cycles and processes of the universe, but the Council knows what you set out to accomplish last time you came before them. They've got you on their files. I don't know why I keep coming back to bureaucratic analogies when I talk about the Council, because pencil-pushers they are not, but nonetheless they know exactly what you said last time.

My belief in this part of the life process stems from the Kabbalistic lore of Tikkunim, which means 'corrections', a word that immediately summons images of you hunched over your primary school desk, your tongue sticking out as you concentrate, busily doing corrections to a drawing or a sum or a little essay riddled with spelling mistakes. But it's an appropriate image, since the corrections that the Council helps us with are all part of our higher education.

As for what you're correcting, the possibilities are endless. Perhaps you were a bad mother, and determined to do a better job next time around. Perhaps you never learnt to express your feelings, and ended up creating hurt and confusion among those you love. Perhaps you're still working off some awful karma picked up lifetimes ago when you were a murdering thug. Whatever it is, you're now approaching the coal-face of the soul, where the hard work lies that will absolve you. That's why I have a problem with the Catholic idea of confession: another human being cannot forgive or negate your sins. Only you – and God – can do that.

Is this all fair? After all, what chance do we have of correcting our flaws if we forget our original goals the moment we're reincarnated? I mean, how can the Council wag its finger at us and point to our original promises, telling us we've only fixed five of the ten problems we set out to fix, when in life we didn't even know we had ten problems? Honestly, who's got time to worry about wiping out bad karma when you've got overdue library books and the in-laws are threatening to descend on you for dinner?

The answer is deeply unsatisfying to our mortal sensibilities: no, we can't remember our goals, but we feel them, as if they are etched onto our souls. And that's why we need to meditate, to be very still and to search for contact with our souls, to know the purpose of our lives and to know what changes we need to make, what problems we need to overcome.

But secret messages etched onto souls just doesn't cut the mustard for many, for whom meditation involves chocolate éclairs and the latest issue of *Cosmopolitan*. These people are trying desperately to find short cuts, trying to get a hotline to that life between lives where we make these decisions and come to these vital realizations.

And the most popular way of doing this is regression, usually under hypnosis. In fact regression is a cottage industry in many places, as people try to access past lives to discover traumas or problems they need to overcome in this life.

The trouble with this is that it short-circuits the natural processes of discovery, and gradually removes your power to change your own destiny, putting it instead in the well-manicured hands of a very expensive therapist or hypnotist. It prevents you from coming to those enormous and yet under-stated realizations – that you have a path to follow, and that you already secretly know that path – and makes you hesitate every time you need to make a decision.

Instead of worrying about what you should be doing (Should I flip a coin? See a psychic? Do a cookery course? If only I knew!), just stop whenever you feel that you have come to a fork in your path, and assess your feelings. You probably do this anyway. But next time, try to listen to yourself without bias or vanity. Also don't over-think your reactions: if a feeling seems too clear, too obvious, don't automatically discard it as wrong or childish. In short, learn to listen to the voice of the subconscious, rather than the voice of the unconscious. You aren't a puppet on a string, jerked this way and that by advice from the outside or mood-swings and doubts from the inside. Learning to listen is one of the most important achievements in our lives, and it takes practice.

Starting again

So you've decided to return to the mortal world, to start afresh at trying to overcome those obstacles or compulsions you've identified with the help of the Council. What now? How do you go from being a spirit 'adult' to being a tiny spark of life, just seconds old? Do you shrink, like Alice drinking the curious liquid after she followed the White Rabbit down the hole? Is there some sort of sudden regression?

If you've read a lot of the books on this topic by various mediums and mystics, you might have encountered the idea of nurseries for the soul, where souls are 'grown' for babies. I'm not kidding; this is what some people believe! Oddly enough they never go into very much detail, so we're still in the dark as to how much fertilizer you need to dump on baby souls to get them to grow. One thing's for sure, though: these authors aren't shy of dumping fertilizer on their readers!

Others describe seriously lame crèches for these baby-souls

(perhaps where they go after they've been worked over by God's combine-harvester?), where the little ones laugh and gurgle and play with balls of light and learn social games. Now I don't know how many of these writers have been parents, but I ask you, would you give your baby a ball of light to play with? It would all end in tears. Or arson.

In other words, certain pop-psychic writers have written a big pile of drivel about this process. They've completely removed the enormous logic from it. Remember, everything in the universe is governed by the great logic of God. (Well, except for politicians.) But perhaps the greatest problem with all of these wild fantasies about babies in divine hothouses is that most souls are *not* babies. Souls can be newly created, or very ancient, but that age has nothing to do with their earthly age. Our life on earth is a split second in the greater process of our soul's progression towards God, and we re-enter earthly lives many times over the course of our soul's journey. In other words, that newborn baby lying there bellowing its tiny lungs out might be a day old or a billion years old, but it is where it needs to be at that moment, where it has chosen to be. It is an 'adult' soul, created in God's image but imperfect, filled with potential but already possessing great wisdom and clarity.

But I'm getting ahead of myself here. Because you're not going to get very far in being reborn if you don't have parents, and this is where you take another enormous stride in your evolution, where you go out on a limb and make a decision that can make or break you. Because *you choose your parents!* It's that simple. You watch, you appraise, you weigh the pros and cons. But you can't carry on shopping around forever, and as with any big decision there comes a moment when you have to take the plunge, for better or for worse.

For many people, it's for worse. And I'm not talking about having to hold Mom's hand to cross the street until you're 25, or

Dad's penchant for going to PTA meetings dressed in alligator-skin pants. I'm talking about genuinely horrible consequences: disease, poverty, abuse. I'm talking about the millions of babies who find themselves in enormous refugee camps, or whose lives are doomed by HIV-infected mothers, or who are born into bloody war-zones.

People sometimes use these realities as an attempt to disprove or challenge the existence of God. How, they demand, can God be kind and all-powerful if He allows innocent souls to be snuffed out like this, or to be born into lives of agony and squalor?

But what this argument fails to accept is that we don't focus on our circumstances or situation when we choose our parents. We choose them by one criterion and one criterion only: their potential as parents. We can't know all possible genetic outcomes. We don't know if we'll be born sickly or crippled, because we can't know: remember, the body is the wild card.

Often we know our parents already. Perhaps the mother we choose was a sister in a past life, whom we know we can trust, who has a great ability to love or nurture. Perhaps our chosen father was our father before, or our son; someone who has proved themselves to be reliable and honourable.

But people change, and souls make mistakes. Just because the man we choose as our father has been loving in the past is no guarantee that he will continue to be so. Being born to abusive parents, or alcoholics, for example, is an unhappy accident, a sudden and unpredictable derailing of all the potential we saw in them from the life between lives.

It is difficult for us to accept that we actively choose certain situations. For instance, why would anyone choose to be born to an HIV-positive mother? What possible value could there be in being orphaned while still a baby, and then clinging on to life for another three or four painful years?

A particularly vicious line of popular spiritual thought tells us that we make these horrific choices in order to learn a valuable lesson. This is a genuinely nasty idea, since it absolves us of all empathy or sympathy for those little children or starving babies who die around the world every day. There is no lesson to be learnt from suffering and premature death. There is no enlightenment in misery. There is nothing godly in being born into a war. These are all the result of a gamble on the part of the soul, a gamble they have, in these cases, lost. They gambled that their chosen parents would love them, give them strong healthy bodies, perhaps carry them out of the horror into a bright future of hard work and slow rebuilding. But they guessed wrong, and death is the result; a return to the drawing board, a return to the Council, and perhaps a more careful assessment next time.

But this doesn't answer why we would choose parents we know have a high likelihood of damaging us by passing on some known genetic problem. For instance, it seems to make absolutely no sense that you would choose a mother with full-blown AIDS. But most decisions are the result of carefully weighing up the odds on either side, and in this case perhaps that mother had something else to offer that was far more important than the gift of a long, normal life. Perhaps she was offering a love not yet experienced, or an outlook on life that was profound and unique. In the final decision, it is possible that these treasures, experienced for only a few months or years, might outweigh a life of lukewarm love and emotional detachment.

Perhaps these ideas seem somehow distasteful to us because we are urged to believe that there is only one life, and only one chance to be happy and successful. We see the death of a baby as a horrible waste, a terrible blemish on the way the world should run. But once you understand the great cycle of reincarnation, and understand the limitless time we have to explore and learn in the Hereafter, a life of eighty years is almost indistinguishable from a life of four days. Right now I'm looking out of my window and watching surfers off Cape Town's Atlantic shore. Some of them are falling off seconds after getting to their knees. Others are riding the big green waves right in to the beach. But all are in the sea, all are happy, all are under the same sun smelling the same sweet air, and all are waiting for the biggest wave, the best wave. In life we fall off, we get dunked, we wipe out; but we always return to swim out to the big swells, and to wait for the next ride.

My own choice was a good example of the risks involved. My father's death was not ordained. I could not know that he was going to die so young. Some mystics would no doubt try to convince me otherwise, that I chose to lose my father so I could become a stronger person, or bring me closer to God, or suchlike gabble. But I know what I chose. I saw a brilliant doctor and someone blessed with exceptional musicality, and wanted that mind. I saw my mother's giftedness as a teacher, and wanted that too.

But the wanting goes both ways. I saw that I was wanted: my parents wanted to give love and share love, and be loved in return by their child.

The birds and the bees ...

We're ready to go. The hard slog and crushing solidity of an earthly life might seem a little daunting, but we're focused and our course is set. We've committed to a new existence, and a new set of actions to be judged by. Finally, with optimism and hope, we've chosen our parents.

Meanwhile, in a crowded restaurant or a small apartment or on a train somewhere in the night it's all happening. Marvin Gaye in the CD player, some vino, some sweet nothings ...

I know, I know, your mother and father never touched each other – you just arrived one day in a brown paper bag. So for the sake of your delicate constitution, let's jump ahead to the moment of conception.

Life has begun, and mum and dad are enjoying a leisurely smoke …

And we're still waiting in the Hereafter.

Remember, just because something is alive doesn't necessarily mean it has a soul. Life can exist without a soul being present. Trees and flowers are alive, but they do not have souls in the way that we understand the idea. Bees are alive, and yet they are not governed by a soul, nor even by a collective soul. They are filled with an elemental spirit, certainly, but not a soul.

The question of when the soul enters the body is an extremely important one, since so much of the raging debate around abortion focuses on this detail. Of course those in favour of abortion are deluding themselves and blurring the cruel realities of this act by trying to find an 'appropriate' age to kill the foetus. They are simply measuring development (and thereby weighing morality) by physical standards: if the foetus still looks like a tadpole, it is not yet a person, and so killing it is far less heinous than killing a tiny person with fingers and toes and hair. But the soul that enters this body is fully formed. Sometimes it is far more learned and experienced than the doctor who is killing its new body.

It is an extraordinary and wonderful experience to 'see' a tiny baby in its mother's womb. I see the energies of new life, the powerful flowing of blood and potential and growth. But before six weeks this is an entirely mechanical or biological process: a five-week-old foetus registers as an organ, a part of its mother. And then like a bolt from the blue the soul is visible, radiating its majesty through that tiny little tadpole. Six weeks, in my experience, is when we arrive. Suddenly the ingredients of life have turned into the ingredients of humanity.

The contrast between the fully formed soul, full of wisdom and humour and knowledge, and the tiny scrap of a body it has chosen, is enormous. I mention humour because often there is a lot of playfulness when the soul enters its new body. We are delighted by our choice of parents and of bodies, but all the same it seems like a big game: if you've ever got hysterical trying to squeeze into a ridiculous fancy-dress costume, you'll know the frivolity that we enjoy at this time. The soul has no physical limits, and so naturally this is not a literal shoehorning of a large mass into a small space, but all the same the soul has become used to the huge scope and enormous freedom of the Hereafter, and slipping into this new little vehicle does seem a touch ridiculous.

The veil rises

Our personas are still intact when we enter the body. We are who we are. We have a certain knowledge of our souls (or as much as we can have on the first level, which really isn't that much!). We sit in the dark, looking forward to a new life, wondering if and how it will be like the ones past, hoping that it will be better or different or longer or shorter. We sit with all these thoughts, all this experience, and we wait. Sometimes we might even contact our parents with a sneak preview: my daughter Aviva visited me early in my pregnancy, showing me exactly what kind of person she would become, introducing her soul to me in all its beauty before it had fully integrated with her new little body.

Slowly these thoughts become less distinct. Slowly they melt into dreams. The soul drifts away from alertness and awareness. For want of a better word, the soul drifts into sleep. Like a powerful drug, this deep sleep sweeps across us, and we hang in a timeless, placeless void, dreaming of the life that is to come, dreaming with love of our parents. It is reassuring, warm, but all suddenly unreal. The certainties of the first level, the wealth of knowledge and experience gained there, slip away as we dream.

The veil of forgetfulness has been drawn over our eyes and

minds. Months from birth, we have forgotten everything about ourselves, about where we came from and where we are going to. The only knowledge that remains is that we are safe for the moment, and that we know our parents.

And then one day all hell breaks loose. Perhaps we are sleeping, perhaps we are hanging about in the darkness feeling a little fidgety, when suddenly we are moving. We are pushing, we are being pushed, and we don't know why. Like being awakened from a deep sleep, we are disoriented, irritated, afraid.

And then we panic, as a sudden realization and memory shoots through us. We realize we've made a terrible mistake. We don't know why, because we can't remember our decision to return to this world and to start a new life. We don't know that it is part of a process, of our own doing. But we are certain for an awful moment that we've taken a wrong turn.

Perhaps because of my abilities, or through some physical complication at birth, the veil of forgetfulness never erased my self-knowledge. I remember so clearly how much I didn't want to be born, how much I resented being shoved so rudely into the light. I remember how comfortable I was, how desperately I wanted to go back to the comfort and the dark and the warmth.

But for most people there is a merciful anaesthetic. At the moment of birth, as you emerge, the veil is completely drawn again. You forget even your panic. It leaves you for the rest of your life. But the residue of that fear remains, a moment of sadness and confusion. And you cry, and your mother hears you for the first time.

However, as we lose one focus, we gain another. The moment we are born, we decide to die. It is a choice we make subconsciously. Birth is traumatic and shocking, we realize. I want to go back. I want to die, and go back to – well, whatever came before this and comes after it. That conviction plants itself deep in the psyche, and it sets the clock counting down.

The deathing impulse is enormously strong, enormously primitive; but we are not slaves to it. In fact there are almost no impulses or deep-rooted desires that we cannot control if we meditate and search ourselves and find some understanding of our motives and desires. I believe that it is possible for us to choose life rather than death. You might have heard of rebirthing, a meditation whereby we are 'walked through' the birthing process; where we revert emotionally to that moment when we chose to die. Films and the media have often portrayed this technique in a fairly unflattering light, and have been negligent or inaccurate in presenting it as a kind of psychotherapy designed to help people overcome childhood traumas or separation anxiety or a host of ailments.

Think about a massage, how great it makes you feel. Or a thorough session of yoga or simple stretching. All you've done is just centre yourself: you've taken a few deep breaths, performed some fairly basic tasks with your body. And yet you feel like a million bucks. You feel athletic, potent, compact. You feel like you could run 100 metres in ten seconds, or at least jog around the block without blacking out or hallucinating!

These are conventional exercises or rituals, widely accepted and regarded without suspicion and cynicism. Well, except for the jogging part: I'm starting to think that the fabled endorphin rush is a lie cooked up by fit people to make unfit people feel worse about themselves! But seriously, even these rituals are meditations of a sort. If you've ever sat on an exercise bike and found yourself lost in thought, only half-conscious of pedalling, then you'll know that meditation takes many forms.

Rebirthing is simply a meditation, and can have many positive effects on mind and body. But perhaps the most important of these is that it can regenerate the soul. Going back to the point where we injected our souls with the slow poison of mortality, perhaps many times, we can learn to make a different choice.

In her book *Science and Health with a Key to the Scriptures*, Christian Scientist founder Mary Baker Eddy documented cases where people seem to have conquered the deathing impulse. In one extreme case a woman even seemed to freeze herself in time. Her fiancé was lost at sea, and every day the grief-stricken girl would get up, go to the window, and gaze out at the ocean. Those who knew her realized that she believed with her whole being that her sailor would return to her. Each day she would watch and wait, her life suspended. When she died at the age of 80, strangers and objective observers were shocked and disturbed at her appearance: she didn't look a day over 21.

Time is not a stream. Time's unstoppable advance is a human creation. Time is an idea. The case of the young old woman suggests that when we stop believing in time, the physical effects of this construction stop affecting us.

This is a fairly extreme theory, I know, but I'm sure that you have already experienced less dramatic examples of how we allow a mere idea – the ticking of a clock – to govern our lives in a very physical way. Have you ever been enjoying an evening with friends, and suddenly looked at the clock and seen that it is midnight when you thought it was 10 pm? How did you feel? The chances are you suddenly felt tired, or at least had an attack of the yawns.

Often, time does awful things to our minds. Remember those final maths exams in high school? Do you remember the last two minutes, how everything seemed to speed up but your ability to think and write slowed down? Whereas two minutes an hour earlier seemed like enough time to work out a particular problem, now it barely seemed enough time to rule a new margin? You sweated, you looked around the room desperately. You fidgeted and flexed your fingers frantically. Just sixty little ticks left on the clock – it seemed like an instant! And yet think of what happens in a minute: death, life, love, fear, relief, discovery.

Sure, a maths exam isn't exactly a life of 80 years. So how about more familiar examples of ageing that you've probably encountered in your own life? Think of the old man, going on for 80, who somehow keeps fathering children (his oldest is 40 and baby's just turned 12!). Think of how he laughs and drinks and swears, how he travels, or how he tells everyone to buzz off because it's time for his siesta. His knees grind and he's got two artificial hips, but he behaves like a 40-year-old.

Now compare him with the pale and fragile 65-year-old, who sighs or who groans every time he stands up. Think of the musty little house, the drawn curtains, the smell of mothballs and the overwhelming mood of decay and decline. Think of how he secretly seems to want to be ancient. He is willing himself to be old and decrepit. His health is fine, yet he surrounds himself with bottles of pills, and whenever he gets a cold he updates his will.

The point is that time is what we make it. And I believe that it is possible to make nothing of it or, said in another way, make it nothing. We can extend our lives by dismissing the idea of time. The limits of this meditation, this lifestyle, are unknown. But is immortality possible? Perhaps.

When it goes wrong

The story of little James Leininger and his World War Two 'flashbacks' is fascinating, but what's wrong with it? Does anything about it strike you as unfair, or perhaps out of kilter with the great checks and balances of the universe as I have been describing them? Well, for starters you could say that in James' case the veil of forgetfulness malfunctioned, as it did with me. But what about the fact that this child is being handicapped in this life by those nagging traumas of a past life? Isn't this a strange case of the sins of the 'father' being visited on the 'son', even though they're the same person? Why should innocent little James have his life rocked by persistent nightmares from the life of an entirely different person?

The answer to all of these questions is an unsatisfying one: sometimes the filters just aren't good enough. In other words, sometimes reincarnation and rebirth just isn't enough.

In James' case I believe that his soul never properly dealt with the trauma of the physical death in 1945. It remained so intense and immense that he carried it through the veil and into his new life.

But surely, you might ask, isn't this a major malfunction? Isn't this sort of thing supposed to be sorted out on the first level? And why did the Council allow such a damaged and traumatized soul to come back?

Well, perhaps now is the time to reiterate a truth about the first level: the Hereafter is not perfect. Remember, it's only one step away from our messy, chaotic, dysfunctional world. The Council makes mistakes. As you'll soon see, there are some souls or entities that the Council is unable to deal with. In fact in comparison with the fifth or sixth or seventh heavens, the universe of recently dead souls and Councillors and suchlike is just as clumsy and chaotic as our world.

So just because you've died, and have discovered that the soul survives death, it is by no means a foregone conclusion that you're going to be able to work through the issues and traumas that plagued you at the time of your death. In our world, therapy doesn't always work. If it did we'd all be ruled by therapist-kings in an emotionally healthy Utopia! And the same applies in the Hereafter: the therapists might be angelic beings or guides, and the self-knowledge might be drastically more accessible and profound, but it still doesn't guarantee that we'll be ready to heal, or even want to heal.

So was James sent back prematurely? It's possible. It's also possible that he fooled the Council because he was fooling himself. Often when we're stressed or traumatized we convince ourselves that we are fine, that we're coping. Perhaps you've done this yourself – gone along through life for a period of weeks or months, not feeling particularly happy but certainly not feeling unhappy. And meanwhile you're just hanging on (even though you keep telling yourself you feel fine), and an implosion is just waiting to happen. Perhaps James' soul had reached this point in the Hereafter. He might have convinced himself that he was ready to start a new life, and in so doing convinced the Council. And so he reincarnated as a healthy, normal baby, and one day out of the blue the cracks started showing.

But there is another more consoling possibility in James' case.

People often believe that the Hereafter is a cure-all. If you are a Christian or a Jew or a Muslim you probably believe that heaven or paradise automatically heals every physical, mental and emotional defect, almost as if the act of dying shunts you through some enormous godly car-wash. You come out perfect on the other side.

This is simply not the case. There is no car-wash, no instant purging and cleansing and healing. There is only a vastly increased potential for self-improvement and self-education. And often the only really effective way of going about those improvements is to come back and to get your hands dirty all over again.

And so it's possible that the Council made no mistake with James' soul, but rather realized that the only thing that could heal his emotional and spiritual wounds was the love of what sounds like a rational and sensible family, a family that would respect his trauma and not try to convince him that he was imagining things or being crazy. It is very possible that James went back precisely when he needed to, and that his nightmares were part of that painful but essential process that we all face in one form or another.

Old souls and other nonsense

Have you ever met someone who seems amazingly 'together', as if they've worked out an awful lot of things about life? Perhaps they're attractive and calm and project a sense of wisdom. Perhaps nothing seems to faze them. Often they're the sort of person you develop a little crush on, simply because they seem somehow sophisticated and at the same time uncomplicated.

If you're like millions of other people out there, you'll have entertained the thought that your new acquaintance is an 'old soul'. It's a phrase that's soaked into our minds from television and agony-aunt columns over the last couple of decades, and it suggests a soul that has been around the block a few times, and has worked out many of life's lessons.

But often the crush or admiration gets in the way of the next logical step. Surely, if this 'old soul' has been around for such a long time, it's doing something wrong? Why, if it's so wise, is it still on this earthly level? Surely it's like being 25 in high school, and not something to admire or be proud of?

The first attitude to dump here is that an advanced soul is 'better' than a less experienced soul. We are instinctively drawn to wisdom and experience, perhaps because in our crude little world, these things helped the fittest to survive. But ideas like 'better' and 'worse' simply don't apply to the development of souls: each soul is where it is, and that's all there is to it. There is no schedule to keep to. There are souls that develop quickly, but they are not 'gifted' or 'precocious'. Souls that take hundreds or thousands of round-trips to discover and fulfil their purpose are not 'slow' or 'backward'.

Some esoteric writers have sucked all sorts of things out of their thumbs about the number of times we reincarnate before we move on (seven is a favourite number, as I've mentioned previously!), but the reality is far simpler and far less contrived. We come back until we catch on, until the light bulb goes on over our heads. And that could be an awfully long time, if you consider the limitless permutations of experiences we can undergo in our lives.

But getting back to these cool cucumbers who wander about with an air of worldly weariness, these old souls: there are always people who have figured out more than you or me, people who seem just a step away from enlightenment and ascension. But there's a simple question you need to ask about them: do they think they know it all? Is it wisdom, or is it ego? If it's ego or arrogance, then the chances are that they're young souls who have become bloated on the little bits of wisdom they've accumulated.

Old souls will never claim mastery of anything. You simply can't be that arrogant or confident when you've experienced so much – how often haven't you heard the phrase 'the more I learn the less I know'? If someone feels they're just one step away from knowing it all, they are immature and blinded by distractions. They're in the kindergarten phase of their soul's evolution, flushed with egotism, that 'look at me!' phase all children go through. And they're allowed to be like that. They are not vain and morally wrong any more than a boasting three-year-old is vain and morally wrong.

Having said that, though, not all behaviour that is natural should always be tolerated. Inexperienced souls feel pretty pleased with themselves, but it doesn't follow that all inexperienced souls feel that way. There are no set phases that we all need to go through, and there are certainly no actions we all need to experiment with to learn or progress. In this world many people experiment with drugs as a 'phase', and then move on, but many people don't. They are no less savvy for having declined a quick snort or drag in a dingy club.

We might not be compelled to try out certain things in each life, but that doesn't disguise the fact that most of us have done some fairly nasty things in past lives. We are not normally predisposed to murder, and taking another human life is certainly not something that we all have to try to deal with along our path, but you'd be amazed at how many of us have killed at one time or another. Yes, and that means you too. It is very likely that right now you are working off the last traces of karma picked up at some time when you bumped someone off. Because I can remember so many past lives, I'm fully aware of what I'm paying reparation for. In the kingdom of the Maya in modern Peru, I used to tear the hearts out of people and chuck them off cliff-tops to appease my gods. But Your Honour, I swear it wasn't murder! I honestly believed I was doing the right thing, even doing those people a favour. I mean, they were going to a better place, and our lands were going to be fertile! It was a win-win situation!

You're right – it's a pretty feeble plea to cop. And believe me, I'm still paying it off today. And the reason I'm still paying it off is that there is always a price for taking a life. If murder was a natural part of life, it wouldn't have a karmic penalty. That's why people who suggest that murderers are acting as instruments of God are dangerously deluded. Every so often a child or some treasured spouse or parent is killed in South Africa and the surviving relatives bravely say that the death and grief are part of God's plan. Unfortunately this is simply not true. You can understand why people destroyed by bereavement would want to find some purpose in their loss, to make the terrible pain and confusion diminish, but murders and murderers have nothing to do with God. God gave us freedom of choice, and just as we can choose good, we can choose evil.

Psychotics and neurotics – the demented dead

A hundred and fifty years ago Europe and the United States were developing incredibly quickly. Steam power and other technical innovations were paving the way for the Industrial

Revolution that would change the world forever. Colonies were being gained and exploited, travel was becoming an affordable luxury, literacy was spreading, and huge breakthroughs in health-care were coming thick and fast.

And yet amid all this progress and civilizing, untold numbers of people were chained up in asylums or institutes, abandoned as 'mad' or 'hysterical' or 'criminally insane'. Medicine might have been advancing, but the final frontier – that of the human brain and mind – was almost entirely uncharted.

Today an echo of this ignorance still resounds. Ask the lay-man to describe a psychotic, and the chances are they will describe an axe-murderer. Ask them to define a neurosis, and they will talk about biting their nails. This is why it is important to discuss these souls in this book, to help clarify their conditions and the process they undergo when they die. But most essential-ly, one needs to understand that psychotics and neurotics are very, very different to psychopaths.

Psychotics suffer from mental illness; they are not evil. They are afflicted by neurological imbalances that can often be helped with medication. Neurotics, on the other hand, are victims of psychological imbalances: neuroses are reactive behaviours, the result of some trauma or emotional tangle not yet processed through therapy or medication. Neither of these groups are pre-programmed for violence. Neither of them are by definition crazed killers.

But a psychopath is something altogether different. The word itself is not widely accepted by the medical community, since it is not a single physical or even mental condition. There are no physical attributes that psychopaths share. Psychopaths cannot be diagnosed in the usual medical sense. In fact the word, as it is used by you and me or in movies, refers more to a kind of violent and crazed behaviour than any physical or mental condition. For instance, if a man were diagnosed as psychotic, and lived a quiet life collecting stamps and watering his plants, never hurting a fly, you wouldn't consider him to be a psychopath. But if an apparently normal clerk in an office, untroubled by any kind of mental illness, suddenly chopped up ten of his colleagues, you would. For the purposes of this book, when I refer to psychopaths I am speaking of those beings who kill, often over and over again, apparently without remorse, and sometimes with a great deal of pleasure.

In the introduction I described how I have the ability to see people's auras, their spirit bodies and, underneath, a visual representation of their souls. I say it's only a visual representation, because I have human eyes and a human brain, and so because my tools are fairly limited I can see only what I am capable, as a human, of seeing. Auras appear in various colours, various shades of light and dark, and various patterns. Diseases manifest a particular pattern. Psychological problems like depression likewise project a different pattern and hue to, say, euphoria or love. Every soul on this planet is surrounded by this busy corolla of information, buzzing and flashing and glowing away as we all work and learn our way through life, as we get sick and get better, become miserable or hopeful.

But I've also seen psychopaths, and they are horribly different. Not because I see disturbing auras or a black shadow around them or any of the things you might expect. I'm terrified of them for one simple reason: I see only blaring red in them. I see no sign of a soul. I see no trace of God. I see only blood and killing and horror.

Perhaps I should take a step back for a moment and follow a psychopath through death. Perhaps he's killed himself, in the strange twilight of emotional detachment that many seem to experience. Perhaps he's been executed in a prison. Perhaps he's died of old age. Straight to the Grey Zones, right? Straight to Purgatory for a long long time?

Wrong.

Somehow – and I don't know how – he slips through to the first level of the Hereafter. Perhaps he avoids the astral darkness because it never crosses his blank mind that he has done wrong. Perhaps he is tormented by nothing more than boredom or the fidgety need to kill again as an attempt to feel some kind of emotion. Perhaps it takes a soul to feel shame and guilt, to experience suffering and remorse and redemption. But whatever the case, he strolls through, mediocre and unremarkable and entirely hollow.

Of course he cannot avoid the Council, but what can the Council do? It has no authority to sling him down to the slumlands, and even if it did, it has no actual physical ability to do so. Only an angel would have that power, to be able to come down to the first level and 'physically' eject the psychopath from the Hereafter. But angels are not bouncers. They have their own tasks and duties, and the Council is on its own.

And so of course the psychopath is sent back to the struggle of our human life. It goes back again and again and again, and learns exactly nothing every time, except perhaps that it genuinely enjoys hurting or killing.

Is this a glitch in the system? Is the Council doing us a disservice by sending these creatures back each time to walk among us? And if they're not souls, what are they? The last question is easiest to answer. From a Kabbalistic perspective, psychopaths are part of the *klippot*, meaning 'the empty shells'. It is a very apt description, since they are a kind of spiritual empty shell, a container that can be filled with either good or evil. God and the forces of good don't use crude, simplistic and limited tools like empty shells: God doesn't need zombies when He has souls and angels and light beings. And so by definition only evil fills these hollow creatures. They are not demons, but they walk in the shadowy borderlands between neutral space and the demonic. They are foot soldiers of those demonic forces, working crudely and rather ineffectually for evil in the eternal battle between good and evil. Certainly the murder of innocent people in this world doesn't seem ineffectual to us: it seems awful, and it is. But in the huge scheme it is a drop in the ocean, and this is why psychopaths are failed creatures, useless to both good and evil. They have no power in the universe, and so they wield the only apparent power they can find: the power over life and death.

Where is Hitler?

In the last chapter I spoke about American president Harry Truman paying the karmic price for his decision to kill tens of thousands of people in Hiroshima and Nagasaki in 1945. But when we discuss mass murder, all names pale into insignificance next to one: Adolph Hitler.

A pragmatic student of history asked me a while ago, 'Why does Hitler always get top billing as history's worst killer when Stalin killed more people? Why do we remember 6 million dead Jews and not 10 or 15 or 20 million dead Russians?'

The answer to this is simple: Stalin exhausted his evil on the Russian people. The Russians took it and took it and took it, for decade after decade. They suffered as perhaps no other people have suffered. Yet in the end Russia and its people survived Stalin. But Hitler died just twelve years into his reign, in 1945. Had he won the war, and ruled supreme over the world until, say, the 1960s, our language and morality would have no way of describing the horror he would have unleashed. It sounds like a simplistic playground game to say that Hitler was more evil than Stalin (along the lines of 'the Terminator can beat up the Alien any day!') but it is true: Hitler had the capacity, the evil and the will to destroy most of humanity. That is why he is remembered. We sense that evil even today. We feel with intuition, with our spiritual feelers, that we escaped the ultimate nightmare because he was killed before he could fulfil his evil potential.

Nothing upsets me more than hearing people describe Hitler as a tool of history. Some Jews even try to rationalize his existence by saying that without him there wouldn't have been a Holocaust and therefore a state of Israel. This is really clutching at straws, but perhaps it's understandable: after all, if God is good, how could He allow someone like Hitler to be born and to thrive?

The answer once again takes us to the edge of worlds, where things slip through cracks, and monstrous evil can shelter in apparently mediocre bodies or souls. You might assume that Hitler was a psychopath gone entirely off the deep end; but Hitler chose evil. He was faced with a choice, and gave it plenty of thought in his youth. His path was determined by his will, by his ambition, by his hatred. He actively pursued occult practices. He learned and schemed and theorized. No, Hitler had a mind and a heart that he deliberately turned to the purpose of killing. In other words, Hitler had a soul, and Hitler still has a soul.

And so we come to another of these great questions about justice in the universe: should some souls simply be punished forever? Are some souls so monstrous that they should not have the right to reincarnate and learn and progress? Aren't even the Grey Zones (where redemption is always possible) far too cushy for these abominations?

I don't know about forever. But I do know that Hitler hasn't been reincarnated. He isn't in the Grey Zones. He is being punished, right now. And his punishment is nightmarish.

When I write it in the way that I am about to, it doesn't seem particularly horrible. In fact it doesn't seem nearly harsh enough to fit his crimes. But let me explain, and then imagine it yourself.

Hitler is trapped in stone. And his soul is screaming.

He is literally trapped in stone, his soul spread through the atoms and electrons of a piece of rock. It is a literal, physical mass of stone – granite, quartz, I don't know – and it is a crushing, infinitely claustrophobic prison. In the spirit realm earthly stone possesses the greatest density of any element or object, and a soul trapped in stone is suffering a torment that you and I cannot imagine.

I don't know where this stone is, but it's not on our planet. Our world is not polluted with his presence any longer. There is no trace of Hitler on earth.

But what equivalent punishment can be meted out to monstrous psychopaths? Hitler had a soul, and can suffer because of that soul, but how do you punish an empty vessel that is impervious to punishment and suffering? Surely something rotten to the core with evil, so completely without the chance of rehabilitation, needs to be removed entirely from the universe?

Anything that can be made, can be unmade. But God is compassionate, and gives infinite chances. I have never heard of a soul being unmade. In fact I don't know what it would take for God to obliterate a soul: both Lucifer and Hitler kept theirs intact. All the same, if God chooses to destroy something utterly, it is done. And sometimes that final destruction is unleashed on an empty vessel, a psychopath. It is removed from the universe; and the endless cycle, the stuck record of reincarnation, is brought to a merciful end.

Reincarnation and race

Jews are taught that they have a Jewish soul, that they stood on Mount Sinai, and that they will stand there again one day. It is an idea that has kept the faith strong, and has helped keep the Jewish people intact despite endless persecution over the last thousand years.

But if my soul is Jewish, how do I account for strong and vivid past-life memories of being the wife of a Bible-thumping missionary in Kenya, pouring out fire and brimstone on hot, still African mornings? Why do I remember being a black African, worshipping the spirits at the shrines of my ancestors? Why do I remember being a Muslim, adhering strictly to the words of the Prophet?

Yes, I've been Jewish in a few lifetimes before this one, but in my experience the soul has no political or religious allegiances. It is not male or female. It is not black or white.

Some of my past lives were far better than others, but this had nothing to do with the race or religion of the body I inhabited at that time. Being pecked to death by vultures in the Tower of Silence while I was a Zoroastrian doesn't really rate as a highlight, but that was all about karma – what goes around comes around – and nothing else.

Man's best friend!

When we're sad they cuddle up against us or lick our faces until we're hysterical. When we go away on holiday they're suicidal. When we come home they're the embodiment of joy and gratitude. Our pets can be our best friends, our most trusted confidants, and our most faithful companions. The loss of a pet, even to natural old age, can fill us with real grief, as sharp and bitter as if we'd lost a good human friend.

If you have dogs or cats or birds, in fact any furred or feathered friend who shares your life and your home, then I'm preaching to the converted. But I can't let this chapter end without addressing a question I am often asked:

Do pets join us in the Hereafter?

Firstly, all living creatures have a spirit world, just as we do. Often it is very different, and on a greatly different scale. For instance plants, which share a group spirit, are not following a spiritual path towards enlightenment: they are already more or less 'perfect' – botanists are welcome to correct me, but I don't think it's possible to come across a dysfunctional shrub! Fish and birds, which are more complex life forms and so have more complex spiritual aspects, nevertheless are not individual enough to possess individual, unique souls. Their reincarnation is often instant, because they share one soul with their flock or school: I can see the little manifestation of a soul around each bird, and I've seen a pigeon killed by a car and watched that soul shoot straight into another bird nearby. It isn't possession, just resettlement!

As we proceed higher up the chain of animal life, individuality and a unique soul becomes more and more evident. Domesticated animals, whose evolution has been so closely linked with ours, are often the most highly developed in terms of this unique spirituality. Pigs are not only extremely intelligent, but have lovely souls and personas. Four pigs might look identical in a barnyard, but ask the farmer and you'll soon discover that Daisy is grumpy, Rumbles is destructive, Ruth is inquisitive and Clover is kind and nurturing. This is why eating meat must be a conscious and carefully considered decision: the mass-murder of these little souls carries a karmic price, and you as the person finally responsible for those deaths will bear some of that burden.

But no animal soul is as closely linked to our own as our household pets, especially dogs and cats. These are species whose entire universe – their bodies, minds, habits, emotions – have been shaped and created by us. People who are uncomfortable around animals sometimes suggest that animals' devotion to us is based on food and fear, but this is nonsense. Our pets love us, just as we love them. Leave your pet next to a heap of food and go away for a few days, and often the animal will ignore the food and simply pine.

So do they join us in the Hereafter? Well, yes and no. Remember, we don't live in the Hereafter for eternity, so there isn't really any place for them to wait for us. But because these are realms where time and space (as we know them) have no authority, they can – and often do – find us during our time in the Hereafter. If we loved them enough, and they felt loved enough, they will wait for us.

However, far more common is reincarnation. We outlive our pets many times over: dogs rarely reach their twenties, and cats can manage only a few years more. And let me tell you, the intensity with which we miss these bright little creatures pales into insignificance next to their longing for us! Which is why they usually reincarnate almost immediately and come back to the family they've left.

It happens every day, all over the world. A family whose trusty old retriever has died decides a few months later that they want a puppy, preferably of the same breed, and they start making inquiries. And you can bet that away in the animal spirit world, a certain little retriever soul is making its own enquiries! Of course we don't always pick that puppy or that kitten who so badly wants to be picked, because there is always risk with reincarnation, as you know. But it happens enough to make it a fairly safe option, and a deeply satisfying one for both owners and pets.

In fact some time ago I was phoned by a woman in floods of tears. Her favourite bulldog, a real character with the heart of an angel and the looks of, well, not an angel, had died, and she was desperate to know about his passing and whether or not he was safe and happy. Almost immediately I was given a message from the other side by a soul I couldn't quite visualize, advising her to travel to a kennel in Rustenburg – way out of Johannesburg where she lives – and to be there on a particular day. I told her the date and the location, and left it at that. A few weeks later she called again: a litter of perfect little bulldogs had been born at that kennel on that day, and she'd recognized hers in an instant, a puppy with identical markings to the one she'd lost. Even its mannerisms were identical. Her dog had come back to her.

So yes! The news is good. They're still going to be in your life for a good long time, demanding treats and laps!

When do you stop?

Round and round and round we go on this great carousel of experience and knowledge, hopefully each time discovering another fragment of our souls for the first time, coming fractionally closer to God. But eventually there comes a point where the last wrinkles have been smoothed out, and the last questions answered. Finally, after what has perhaps been a thousand years, you are ready to leave behind the universe of reincarnation. It is time to leave the earthly plane and the first level forever. Suddenly the retirement village of the Hereafter, the Council, all of it, is gone. You have transformed into a new being, shedding your spirit body. This little body, so long your friend and protector, falls away and decays, and returns to the nothingness that it was made from. You are no longer in any body, no longer recognizable to our limited human consciousness ...

But you're jumping the gun here. Because you're not going anywhere until you've hit the books. Remember the choice presented by the Council so long ago? Live or learn, the awesome decision we make after reviewing our lives. We've lived – plenty. But now it's time to go back to school.

The Halls of Learning

Time to hit the books

The wisdom we gain through experiencing life is invaluable. From the moment we start putting things in our mouths as babies until the day on which we smell our last flower or hear our last piece of gossip (God willing as a great-grandparent!) we are soaking up information and wisdom like an enormous sponge. It is sometimes a valuable exercise simply to sit still for a moment and think of all the things you know through experience: not just the big things, like how to run a business or raise a family, but everything – how you know when it's going to rain, how you manage to walk to your toilet in the pitch dark without stubbing your toe; the sort of trivia that you take for granted.

But if life held all the answers we'd all be geniuses. The School of Hard Knocks is well and good, but unfortunately there isn't a University of Hard Knocks to which people can graduate. In other words, in this life and the next we simply have to go to a more formal, academic source for knowledge.

These are realities of the modern world. Brain surgeons don't start as apprentice brain surgeons. You can't teach yourself nuclear physics in your spare time. Even more creative skills, like writing or playing musical instruments, demand formal training if we're ever going to do them properly.

We have had elite institutions of learning for as long as people have sought knowledge. In the beginning they took the form of secret societies, where shamans or gurus initiated a chosen few into their ways. The ancient Egyptians had libraries, schools and even places of higher learning that we would recognize as the predecessors of universities. The Greeks, when not lost in furious philosophizing or running marathons in the nude, gathered in amphitheatres to listen to the theories of academics. Islamic thinkers pushed the boundaries of scientific discovery, making breakthroughs in mathematics, astronomy and medicine; and away to the east the Chinese were perfecting technologies that Europe took another 500 years to master.

The Dark Ages threatened to snuff out the light of learning across much of Europe, but the new bearers of that divine light, the monks and religious scholars of Christendom, retreated to new institutions, in Paris and the English countryside. A thousand years later the Universities of Paris, Oxford and Cambridge still impart the wisdom of our tribe, revealing knowledge that once would have seemed not only mystical but deeply heretical!

We are *Homo sapiens* – Thinking Man. Yes, we're also Killing Man and Stupid Man and Planet-Destroying Man, but these are a result of drifting away from self-knowledge, and the dimming of our vision of God. I mean really, if we are here just to eat and sleep and have children and thump each other on the head – as some existentialists like to say between long sighs – then why do we have this miraculous thing in our skulls? The human brain is far and away the greatest wonder of the natural world, and we certainly didn't develop it just by eating our wheaties!

So what would you think the next logical step to be, after

death? Would it make sense for us to pass over to the first level and suddenly – pop! – become imbued with the great secrets of the universe? Of course not! Dying is an important part of life, but doesn't earn us instant intellectual frequent flyer miles. Death is a beginning, not a destination. As in life, we need to continue learning.

And let me tell you, it can be a real drag. Remember, when we cross over into the Hereafter we're still essentially us: well-intentioned, aware of what we need to do, but a little too keen on rest and relaxation. It's not made any easier by the initial period of rest and adjustment we experience immediately after dying, especially if we've manifested a blissfully peaceful reality for ourselves. I mean, would you want to heave yourself up out of a favourite window seat or garden bench, where sunbeams were gently warming you and leaves were dappling the light across your book or magazine, and trudge away to school? Would you have the resolve and energy to fling yourself into an entirely new course of study when all you wanted to do was snooze for eternity?

But we're at this point because we've chosen to be. We've gone before the Council, who have reminded us of all the decisions we made, and shown us all the resolutions we fulfilled or forgot about. We have thought long and hard about the value of returning to the earthly world in new incarnation. But in the end we've decided that we need to study further. Reincarnation sounds very appealing, but we are just self-aware enough to realize that without greater insight and wisdom we're very likely to repeat our old mistakes again. And trust me, you don't want to go before the Council like a sheepish schoolboy and be told you haven't made a single correction or achieved a single one of your objectives …

There are a handful of moments in our lives that reverberate and resound because of their majesty and awe. Perhaps the birth of a child; a staggering flash of insight about some crippling problem; a particular image that burrows straight through our minds into our souls. Think of the moments in your own life that stand out like sunbeams across a rainy landscape. They are moments that you will never forget. Perhaps your memory of them might alter or fade a little, or in old age you might remember them quite differently to the way they actually happened, but their essence is unforgettable.

It's about to happen again.

No soul can enter the Hall of Learning and not be profoundly altered. It seems a little facetious to say that it is a religious experience, since this is all happening in the afterlife, but that is the sense one has when you realize that you are facing the ultimate University, the library that contains all knowledge, and all possible knowledge. Birth, death, the discovery that the soul survives death, our first glimpse of God's power, and our first few tentative steps into the Halls of Learning: these are immense moments in our lives.

'The Halls of Learning' is a rather melodramatic phrase, I know. Esoteric writers don't always come up with the best names for the things they have seen, and I'm sure, if Will Shakespeare or George Orwell had been psychic, they would have coined a far more imposing term. But it's the one we've got, so I'll stick with it for now.

By now you know that much of what we see in the Hereafter is a projection, an idea created by the need to be surrounded by things that we recognize. The same applies to this profound experience of learning we are about to embark on. The Halls of Learning take on an infinite number of forms, giving each soul an image or concept that that soul can comprehend and not feel threatened by.

For example, if you arrive from the Western Tradition in search of knowledge, you're going to be expecting something like a University. And that's what you're going to see: tremendous marble pillars, huge corridors in quiet, peaceful libraries, tranquil little gardens in courtyards. If you arrive from, say, a rural Xhosa or Zulu tradition, you are likely to see a kraal or initiation school. Some cultures have no institutions of higher learning or insight, but rely on oral traditions or simple person-to-person contact, perhaps sitting around a fire in a great open desert, or in a snow-covered hut on the tundra. These souls will experience their own intellectual awakening through a familiar figure, perhaps a father or a respected uncle or chieftain. But all of us recognize this place for what it is: the storehouse of universal wisdom.

Again I'm being too literal. The Halls of Learning, in whatever shape they appear, are not found in a literal place. There is no *place* in the Hereafter, no physical space. I'm going to use the analogy of the Internet in this section, and perhaps this is a good time to start. The Internet contains a huge amount of knowledge. Of course this knowledge is often lost or hidden in a monumental heap of online rubbish, but still, just by sitting in front of a screen for half an hour you can have the sort of overview of world events the ancients would have reserved for their gods. You can read the classics, see live footage of any part of the world, predict the weather, and learn how to make anything from brownies to bombs.

So, the rubbish apart, the Internet is an extraordinary store of knowledge. But the Internet doesn't live anywhere. There isn't a room somewhere with a sign on the door that says, 'Keep out, Internet at work'. If you're struggling to imagine the Halls of Learning as not being a solid marble building floating in space somewhere, just think of the Internet, how it's always humming and buzzing around us.

It's interesting how literal we become when we study or learn. Many people need to see letters on a printed page before they'll take something in. I have a friend who hates reading off a computer screen, because he says he likes the feel and smell of paper pages, and the small sense of achievement he feels every time he turns a page. Other people need diagrams or practical examples to understand an idea. And so it's a natural reaction for you to be imagining a huge library containing a million books or a million computers.

But because everything is a projection, if it's a million books you want, it's a million books you'll get. A wise man who died, say, three thousand years ago, would probably imagine that all the knowledge in the universe could be contained in ten thousand scrolls, and so he'd find a library or a cave or a monastery containing those ten thousand scrolls. If he suddenly found himself in a neon-lit library made of glass and steel and faced with a million buzzing computers, he'd no doubt think he was in hell. We get what we're ready to get.

'Unputdownable! So good, it was like being there!'

We've all had the experience of reading an unputdownable book or watching an enthralling film or being led from one fascinating Internet link to another. Time seems to slow to a stop, and you are entirely drawn into the material you are experiencing. Often when we put down a book or the end credits roll in the cinema, we feel a kind of jolt of reality as we return to our own minds and lives from far away. (The Internet saves its jolt for the end of the month when the phone bill arrives ...)

The experience of learning in the Hereafter, of accessing the infinite wisdom in the universe, also known as the Akashic Record, is much the same. We project a person or scroll or book or screen, in fact any interface we are comfortable with, and at once we are absorbed by what we encounter. It's interesting how, in our daily lives, we say that we were absorbed by something, when so often it is we who are doing the absorbing. And freed of our physical brains and all the literal and spiritual distractions of this life, we absorb everything. Or at least, everything that we're allowed to, but I'll get onto this shortly.

Think of a time when you can remember the actual experience of learning; a time when you were entirely focused on a new world of knowledge, and you felt that unique sensation of having your mind expanded. Got something? Now, what did you think of? Sitting in front of a pile of books in the wee hours of the morning, reaching for the sixth cup of coffee?

Or did you think of an experience, a few minutes or hours of discovery when you walked on a mountain or fought with greasy sparkplugs or pored over an instruction booklet badly translated from the Koran? The chances are you thought of an experience rather than a studying session. Because true learning comes only through internalizing knowledge, and we internalize knowledge far more quickly and easily by experiencing something new. Most guidebooks about Turkey will explain how to haggle for a rug. You read the section, remember one or two key phrases, and that's that. But do you know how to haggle in a sweaty corner of Istanbul? Of course not. Until you've been yelled at by three competing carpet salesmen, all offering you their sister and first-born if you'd only buy their product, with hands waving and surly shrugs suddenly turning into new, fractionally reduced offers, you don't have a clue.

I'm not saying that reading isn't important. It is fantastically important, and parents who don't read to their children are handicapping them severely. But the best learning is experiential. And so is our experience of the Akashic Record. It sounds corny to compare it with a virtual reality environment, but that's the closest experience we've got on the earth plane. Again it might sound silly, but you can go on field trips to understand anything you want. What was Mozart battling with in the early hours of a wintry Salzburg morning? Who thought and said what at the Wannsee Conference when the Nazis sealed the fate of six million Jews? How did people live in Ancient Rome? How did Aztec ceremonies unfold? What did it smell like at the Battle of Waterloo? What did Cleopatra really look like? Why did your high-school sweetheart dump you despite that box of chocolates and the new aftershave? All these answers can be gained just by travelling to each particular moment.

I didn't say 'each particular moment in time' because there is no time or space on the next level. Those moments are instead projected in their entirety in the Akashic Record. You don't travel through time, because all events, all thoughts, everything, are in the same place – ironically, no place – in the Halls of Learning.

Isn't this a huge contradiction? Didn't I say, a few paragraphs back, that some things can't be learned except through experience? If experience is so great, why don't we just reincarnate all the time and skip the Halls of Learning?

Let me clarify this. The best *kind* of learning is experiential, but that doesn't mean we will have all those learning experiences in our concrete earthly lives. We can read about landing on the moon, but we can never really know what it was like unless we've done it ourselves, felt it ourselves, fumbled that often-practised line ourselves: 'That's one small step for man ... I mean *a* man, Houston ... one small step for *a* man, one giant leap for ... oh, hell, Houston, can we take that from the top?'

And even those complex skills I mentioned, which we need to study in this life, only really sink home into our subconscious once we've begun doing them. Yes, you need to study and master abstract theory to become a brain surgeon, but the best or most profound learning starts once you begin operating on real people, in real pressure situations, with real consequences.

The Akashic Record gives us the best of both experiences. It combines the theoretical or abstract with an almost literal experience, planting that new knowledge into our minds instantly and permanently.

Access denied

What would you want to know if you could access the Akashic Record right now? I believe most people would go straight for the big questions: Does God exist? Is there life after death? Is my family safe and happy on the other side? But we've already answered these questions, and in any case, if you're accessing a heavenly store of knowledge, that should be answer enough!

But what next? How do you possibly know where to start, when you can't even imagine the sort of things you don't know? Well, then, how about starting big but vague. Right: Please tell me all the secrets of the universe. Yes, that's what I want! Tell me why God made us, why evil exists, how the world will end, how the universe will end. Let me just make a sandwich, and then we can start …

Not so fast. You're over-reaching. You know it, and more importantly, God knows it. But that's what we do, as people. We're greedy, rash and impulsive. It seems a little harsh to use those kinds of words to describe a desire for knowledge, but not all knowledge is good. More importantly, there is knowledge or wisdom that is simply beyond us at this point. Babies learn instinctively, but that's no reason to give them an encyclopaedia for their first birthday. Luckily babies are shielded from certain knowledge – death, war, hatred, ugliness – by nurturing homes and their inability to interpret language. Although their brains and minds are working furiously, they are still largely unfocused on the world beyond their senses. Children and adults, on the other hand, do not have these shields. We can be traumatized by information we are not equipped to handle, just by switching on a television and seeing something horrible.

As you know, I believe that all human knowledge should be shared, and that the secrets of the universe are not meant to remain secrets. Nothing should be off limits, especially in this world, just for the sake of being mysterious or exclusive. But learning takes time, and we must be very careful of rushing towards revelations and experiences for which we are simply not ready.

In Melville's *Moby Dick*, a little cabin boy called Pip falls overboard during a whale hunt, and is accidentally left behind. It is a bright and calm day, and he treads water for an hour or two until his accident is discovered and he is rescued. An apparently mundane incident, one might think, with Pip none the worse for wear apart from being a little soggy and cold. But when Pip is found, he is mad. Alone in the vastness of the ocean, he has experienced how insignificant a single human life is compared to the vastness of the world. He has seen, with his mind's eye, the face of God in the huge depths below him, and his mind has snapped under that weight. As Ishmael, the book's famous narrator says, 'man's insanity is heaven's sense', and for the rest of his life little Pip is pitied as a madman.

This is a piece of fiction, but humanity's greatest truths are described in great fiction. Pip saw things, understood things, that his mind simply could not contain. That is why God has arranged for us to be shielded from the awesome knowledge of the universe, and why we are allowed to experience it only in small increments.

The first time I saw a soul controlling a body, I thought I was going to die. I thought to myself: a person can't see this and be allowed to live. I've been fortunate in that the restrictions imposed on me are slightly fewer than on most people, and I'm very glad and grateful that I haven't yet encountered anything that has crippled my brain (except for income tax return forms).

So is there knowledge available to us here in the everyday world that would cause us to lose our minds, or worse? A psychologist would probably say that it all depends on what you call 'losing our minds', and whether or not we're emotionally equipped to deal with different realities. After all, we've built up a powerful shield of denial and resignation as it is. We know that there are hundreds of nuclear warheads floating around in the world unaccounted for; we know that the planet no longer has the resources to sustain our species at its current rate of consumption; we know that it's only a matter of time before a vicious virus like Ebola develops an airborne strain and wipes out millions. And yet we go on having children and saving money and going on holiday. How can we live so normally in the face of such doom? Easy. We pretend it isn't there. We block it out. We put up shields, and believe the shields protect us.

But what I'm wondering is if there is anything out there that could get through that shield, despite our best efforts. It would be hard to research this, since anyone who had experienced something mind-destroying would of course be a gibbering wreck in an institution, and thus not a very credible witness. But every so often a story drifts to the surface, and I think such stories are worth taking seriously.

For example, in the early years of the 20th century a rumour started doing the rounds about a passage written in Sanskrit, the ancient alphabet of India, which had the power to kill whoever read and understood it. Most academics and linguists poohpoohed the idea, but one Russian linguistics scholar was fascinated by the legend. In the early 1920s a major language conference was hosted by the Russians, and the scholar announced that he was going to read out the passage, and warned all those who believed the legend to leave the room. He was met with gales of laughter and boos and catcalls, but he persisted. Slowly and deliberately he read out the passage to the uncomprehending and derisive audience. Nothing happened, and he walked from the podium. The next day he was found dead, without a wound or trace of foul play.

Did he prove his point, if a tad too emphatically? Or did he die of embarrassment, as cynics would no doubt suggest? I haven't seen the autopsy report personally, so I can't pin my reputation on it either way, but theoretically it is very possible that he exposed himself to meaning and implications with which he was not equipped to deal.

Think of it this way. There are pieces of information or words that exert an effect on us. I love you. I hate you. You're beautiful. You're hideous. Marry me. I wish you'd die. All words sit on a sliding scale of impact, with mundane comments at one end – 'I'm just popping out for some milk' – and those more emotive ones at the other end. But it seems possible, even probable, that the scale extends on and on, past 'I love you' and 'I hate you' to ideas and words so loaded with meaning, so life-changing, that our brains simply cannot manage them any more.

And back at the Halls of Learning, you've just discovered that there are limits. Perhaps, in your physical interpretation of the space you're in, you discover that shelves A to E are roped off, a polite but firm message to you to turn around and look elsewhere. To turn to the useful analogy of the Internet once more, you've clicked on a link, and suddenly a Net Nanny warning pops up. The Net Nanny isn't God, but merely His machinery working as it has worked since the beginning. You can forge your parents' credit-card details and lie about your age all you like: this is one cyberguard who isn't letting you through.

So how do you progress? How do you get the passwords to those areas that are off limits? As you now know, most of the universe is vibrational, and as soon as we become attuned to certain vibrations, we experience the hidden things that exist there. You've actually experienced this in your own life, when you've been battling with a mental challenge, and suddenly you've just 'got it'. It's an almost tactile sensation of something having changed. Sometimes your skin crawls or your eyes widen. Of course this is a crude earthly experience of a vibrational shift, and when we have learned enough and gained enough insight to be allowed more knowledge in the Hereafter, the vibrational change is more dramatic and profound.

In other words, you don't get the passwords from angels or guardians or guides. You don't wait at the little ribbon blocking a particular passage until some helpful archangel arrives to cut it with a flaming sword (always with the overkill, those arch-angels!). You earn the right to progress. Or more accurately, you gain the strength and perspective to cope with progression.

Saving us from ourselves

Within the boundaries set by the 'passwords' we're given, we are free to study anything we wish; but this doesn't mean we're free to over-indulge in that learning. Remember, just because we're in the Hereafter it doesn't mean we're any less prone to idleness than in this life!

If you've been to university, or have children who have, you know the drill. The student arrives at the hallowed halls, fresh from twelve gruelling years of school. His parents have filled him with inspiring speeches about reaching his full potential and the wonderful life that awaits, but if he's like most students, he's just there to get a piece of paper that allows him to be employed. So, like many of his friends, he decides to do a degree majoring in basket-weaving, surfing (don't laugh – it's already a legitimate subject at a particular American college) and film-making so he can blackmail his father into buying him a digital video camera. Yes, sir, he reckons he's got it all figured out. It's going to be a breeze. This studying stuff isn't so hard after all!

And then along comes his godfather or uncle.

'Ahem, Junior, you might want to reconsider,' says the killjoy, pointing out that while basket-weaving introduces one to other lovely and outgoing basket-weavers, it's not really going to put one's future children through school or set them up in life.

A few pages ago I asked you what you'd study if you could

access the Akashic Record right now. Did you have a moment of confusion or at least indecision, where you seemed suddenly overwhelmed by the choice on offer? If you died today, you might be visiting the Hall of Learning by tonight, or maybe it would only be in ten years from now. But you wouldn't be very different from how you are right now. That indecision and confusion would still be there.

I will discuss guides in a future chapter, but suffice it to say for now that they are souls who, very basically, help us to make the right choices in the Hereafter. And these guides often accompany us to the Halls of Learning, just to help us focus on what we're doing there. If you always wanted to understand why you never seem able to finish anything you start (in any life!), or why your relationship with your children was unhappy, you shouldn't be sidetracked by juicy insights in Medieval politics or trends in the London property market. The guides are there to nudge us towards what we need to be studying and away from the fascination of unlimited knowledge.

So far I've talked about information that we shouldn't have because we're not ready for it; and information we shouldn't access because if we did we'd merely be procrastinating. But the 'passwords' and the guides save us from ourselves in a third, far more profound way.

The Halls of Learning contain all knowledge. A short sentence, easily read and easily passed over. But what does 'all knowledge' mean? Simply, it means all knowledge that has existed, does exist and will exist. Everything. But more than this, it is all knowledge that could possibly exist.

If you've ever watched an episode of Star Trek you might have encountered a science-fiction stalwart, the idea of parallel universes. In a layman's nutshell, this theory (which, incidentally, is not only the preserve of sci-fi fans but is being studied intensively by several physicists and philosophers around the academic world) suggests that there is an infinite number of universes. They don't literally sit in parallel – the mind starts to boggle when we think about the space that would involve – but rather sit parallel in time. And at every moment, in every one of those universes, any number of events is possible, and each one of those possibilities happens.

Let me use a practical example. You're sitting reading this book, and suddenly you hear a screech of tyres, a crash and the sound of breaking glass. Now there is an infinite number of things you could do. You could stand up and run to the window, or you could carry on reading. You could phone a friend, or stand on your head or sell your house or divorce your spouse or have a drink, etcetera etcetera and so on into infinity.

But of course each of those options also has an infinite number of possibilities attached to it: if you ran to the window you could look out, jump out, break the glass, go back to the place you were sitting, etcetera. Do you see suddenly that a huge tree of possible events is growing, each branch splitting into an infinite number of possibilities?

Now, sitting reading, you see them only as possibilities, and when you make your first choice (whether it was to go to the window, or to stay sitting) you might think that all the other possibilities fall away and become irrelevant. But the theory of parallel universes suggests that every single one of those branches exists in another universe. Right now there are an infinite number of you's. Many millions of them are sitting reading this book right now, but many millions more are sleeping or gardening, or chained up in prisons, or working in factories. And in trillions of universes, you simply don't exist. Because if you believe that there are an infinite number of possibilities for the future, you have to realize that you have arrived at this point from an infinite number of possibilities in the past.

In other words, there are millions of universes in which

Genghis Khan sacked Europe and colonized the West; where an asteroid obliterated earth a million years ago; where Hitler was accepted to the art academy and vented his fury and ego on the canvas instead of on the Jews of Europe. And on a far less grand scale, there are millions of universes in which you didn't go to the bookshop and see this book; where you were run over by a bus yesterday, where your parents never met and never had you. Each one of these is as real as the universe you are sitting in right now.

Now I don't know about you, but I could spend an eternity just watching those lives from my vantage point in the Halls of Learning. It would be like the ultimate reality show, with never-ending action and infinite scope for scandal and intrigue! Each one of these possible universes, every single detail of every one, is recorded in the Akashic Record. Thank goodness for guides who'll grab the remote and switch off the telly!

But the time-wasting potential of voyeurism is fairly insignificant next to the dangerous possibilities of seeing our own futures.

If you knew your own future, how would it affect you? If you saw that you were going to die young, or live to a ripe old age surrounded by wealth and happiness, wouldn't you stop trying, stop working hard, stop caring? And likewise if you saw a million futures for yourself, wouldn't you feel totally insignificant, as if it wouldn't matter at all if you simply dropped out of the human race?

Both are very real dangers, and entirely in tune with human nature. It's one of the reasons I can't see my own future or the futures of my children: I just wouldn't be able to function normally knowing anything about these, good or bad. If I saw good things in their future, I might stop worrying about them or pushing them to succeed. If I saw bad things, I'd run with them, try to hide them from danger and grief, and we'd end up being miserable fugitives from our own lives.

Fate or chance?

It's an ancient debate, with people on both sides, ranging from philosophers to drunks leaning on bars (although how often they seem to be the same person!). It is frustrating and compelling, and usually ends with the debaters shrugging and walking away. But it's a question we have to address, given the existence of the Akashic Record: *If every possible outcome is recorded and therefore known by God, doesn't that mean that everything is predetermined? And if everything is predetermined, how can we have free will?* In Kabbalah we face this contradiction often. We learn that we have been given free will, but ultimately God knows what we're going to do. And now for the big contradiction: *There is an infinite number of predetermined courses.* I know philosophers will cringe at this, and accuse me of trying to have my cake and eat it. But this is the great conundrum of fate and chance. In the end we have to admit that our future is predetermined, ordained by God. But in practice there are so many variables that it becomes irrelevant that each course is predetermined. In the final analysis we have been given free will to make one of an infinite number of fixed choices.

Knowledge junkies!

No film, play, novel or computer game can come close to rivaling the immense pleasure and inspiration we gain from a visit to Halls of Learning. We are engrossed, enlarged, enlightened, entertained. There is no earthly experience that can compete for sheer wonder.

That's why the experience of absorbing and being absorbed by the Akashic Record can become addictive. After all, this is what many people have dedicated their whole lives to achieving, and when their guides or other souls warn them about addiction, many express that old earthly cop-out: If it feels so good, how can it be wrong?

You now know that the first level of the Hereafter is not a cure-all or a place where we suddenly find ourselves to be perfect; but can it be so similar to earth that we find ourselves developing new negative issues, new obsessions, that need to be worked through or purged afresh?

The answer is yes, and addiction to knowledge is a good example of this. Souls who are selfish or compulsive, or need affirmation or power, can find themselves becoming enslaved by the rush of infinite and instant learning, and they become distracted from what they are there to do. They ignore their guides, turn their backs on their chosen process of growth, and abandon themselves to this vicarious thrill-seeking.

It seems perverse that souls sometimes need to be cleansed of issues picked up in the Hereafter, but it happens, and the treatments are well defined. Souls can be reincarnated, instantly weaned off that stream of wisdom, but this doesn't usually help: it's fairly pointless coming back to our world of ignorance and confusion to learn how to deal with unlimited knowledge! But perhaps they are sent back more as a punishment than a course of therapy.

The other option for these souls is service. To bask in knowledge is to be self-indulgent. It becomes a selfish pleasure. But the reality of both this world and the next is that we are given abilities and talents that we have a duty to use in order to help others. No man is an island, the saying goes, and this is profoundly true. It is our responsibility as human beings to contribute our talents to the good of the tribe. Akashic junkies need to be reminded of this, and are often compelled by councillors or angelic beings to become guides themselves.

But moderation is everything. There are souls who go to the other extreme, exhausting their talents for the good of others, but with strangely unhealthy motives. We've all met people pleasers, who give and give and give and never ask for anything in return.

We might think they are lovely people or altruistic souls, but often they are driven either by a selfish desire to be liked or valued, or else by a sort of martyr complex, which means they are denying their value as people. Both groups think of themselves as servants but neither understands that service is about taking as well as giving.

Service takes many forms, and in the end our contribution to humanity will be judged. If you're wealthy you're going to have to face a spiritual auditing team. No doubt you will be asked a very simple question, but one that we must all face and answer in this world: how could you so happily amass so much money and so many possessions, when you are fully aware that half the world's population lives on less than $2 a day? Likewise if you have a great intellect but use it only for your own enjoyment and ego, you'll have to explain why you did that, and trust me, you'll get nailed.

I possess knowledge of the survival of the soul. I know that life goes on, and that we are all on a path towards God. For whatever reason, I have been granted this knowledge, and I understand that it is my duty to tell people what I know. In the introduction to this book I mentioned that I resisted this calling earlier in my life. I didn't want to spread this gospel, because it was emotionally hard and practically inconvenient. And that refusal came back to bite me very quickly.

But don't share your gifts because you have to. Don't do it because there's some big celestial stick hanging over you. Do it because you are a human being, aware of other human beings. And do it because it feels so good! If you have enough money to buy this book, you have enough money to roll down your window at a traffic light and give the woman begging with her baby a R50 note. Try it, and see how good it feels to realize that you've drastically altered a stranger's day for the better.

Genius and mediocrity

It's only fitting, when talking about the great store of knowledge that awaits us, to discuss the earthly manifestation of divine knowledge: genius. Science is still arguing about where it comes from and what makes a genius. Is it hereditary? And if so, why did so many genii have quite ordinary parents, very ordinary siblings, and downright dim children?

For example, Mozart's parents were musical but not exceptional. We know very little about their own parents, so it seems there was no particularly noteworthy talent back up the generations. Mozart's own children have disappeared from history, clearly mediocre themselves. So where did the great composer come from?

There is one school of scientific thought that is trying to link genius with mental illness. A study released in 2004 found that many of the 20th century's greatest jazz musicians suffered from a variety of mental disorders, from schizophrenia to depression to epilepsy. It's a desperately depressing theory, since it takes all the mystique out of genius, and suggests that in order to be exceptional you need to be slightly off your rocker.

But suddenly little Pip comes to mind, floating in the Pacific, and Melville's words seem strangely comforting: 'man's insanity is heaven's sense'.

Of course I'm not denying that geniuses might have some mental 'defect' in common. Even Mozart, it is suggested, suffered from Tourette's syndrome, which might account for the curious contrast in his music: on the one hand he reflected the calm and immense beauty of God in his music like no-one, to my mind, except for Johann Sebastian Bach, and yet this was the same composer who crammed his music with almost hysterical frivolity and wrote some wickedly lewd lyrics! But too often science stops looking as soon as it finds something it can understand. For instance, I have been diagnosed with temporal-lobe epilepsy, and doctors will tell you, 'That's why she thinks she sees dead people, why she thinks she can talk to God.' But what if I'm right? What if everything in this book isn't a hallucination? What role does my epilepsy play in my ability? Why does it take a 'defective' brain to trigger the musical genius of Billy Holiday or Mozart? Science needs to catch up with me, not prescribe drugs that reduce me to a known quantity. I respect scientists, and I am fascinated by many scientific processes, but too many seem to have forgotten the wonder and inexhaustible exploration – of *all* possibilities – that lie at the heart of their discipline.

I happen to know that Mozart's ability came from his past lives. His was a soul saturated with music and conflict, and his parents had almost nothing to do with that. He selected them purely to be in a culture and socio-economic group that would allow him to continue his musical ambitions with relative success. Perhaps he was too obsessed with his music. Certainly his fairly reckless private life and his addictive personality suggest that he still had a very long way to go on his particular path. But we should be grateful that he floundered around in this world long enough to leave us the music he received directly from God. His middle name was no coincidence: Amadeus, 'from God'.

Genius is a process. It is the manifestation of a very special history of past lives, and a lucky history: the soul that possesses genius has made the right choices, whether through being educated or by luck, and has not been hijacked by unforeseen catastrophes like murder or the old wild card, a defective body.

You might ask why there aren't more instances of genius. After all, if all you need is luck, why aren't the millions of lucky souls out there also genii?

Of course this is an understatement. We are not supposed to criticize those less fortunate than ourselves, but there are an awful lot of people out there who are neither clever nor intelligent. And I'm not talking about the lack of education that comes from being born into poverty or war. Ignorance and illiteracy are no reflection of a person's intelligence: throughout history simple people, with no schooling at all, have shown tremendous insight and common sense. No, I'm talking about thick-skulled nitwits, who know nothing about anything, least of all themselves.

But even this group is a minority. The great mass of humanity is simply mediocre. It doesn't aspire to greatness, and it does not recognize greatness when it sees it. It crucified Jesus Christ. It said Mozart used too many notes. It never bought a single painting from Van Gogh while he was alive.

Mediocrity takes many forms. Perhaps when I talked of the 'mass of humanity' you pictured the vast crowds of India, or the sprawled metropolises of Nigeria, or the chaos of Mexico City. But mediocrity isn't caused by poverty. The enormous middle classes of the United States and Western Europe are overwhelmingly mediocre. These are people who aspire to own enough money to be able to go on holiday every year. They want to be remembered, but they don't know how to do or make anything memorable. Their awareness of God extends as far as the information they've been told to believe. Of course there are exceptions – there are always exceptions – and among this mass are writers and thinkers and ordinary people who do extraordinary things.

But true greatness, with genius as its pinnacle, is often crushed by that suffocating mediocrity. Who knows how many Mozarts have been forced into the family business, whether it be blacksmithing in China or a firm of attorneys in New York?

Of course genius also depends largely on the times. Shakespeare had a soul that was profoundly aware of humanity and the magic of theatre and words, but he was born at a time when the English language was going through enormous change. The absence of order and rules often leads to anarchy, but it can also lead to extraordinary ambition, and Shakespeare embraced the freedom that was running through the language.

Genii sometimes take rules to their furthest possible point – Mozart was never original, but simply perfected the music that was already in existence – but sometimes they break those rules with startling effect. And if there's one thing the masses don't like, it's people who rock the boat. Comfort and obscurity are the two things most important for mediocre people, and they are easily threatened by people in their family or their culture who begin to stand out.

We call it 'tall poppy syndrome', this curious desire the public feels to build up heroes and then cut them down. It is a limiting human reaction. Perhaps this is what happens when you teach children that everyone is equal, that they're talented and beautiful and priceless. As they grow up they see people who are more talented or beautiful than themselves, and others who are less so, and they smell a big lie. It is hurtful and confusing, and they lash out at those who have revealed this truth to them: the exceptional achievers.

What kind of ideology does this lead to? What are we being told by those who feed our opinions, who encourage us to think this way or that? Perhaps the most obvious – and pernicious – idea being drilled into our heads, is that the most important thing in life is to be a good person. Even among esoteric writers, or those who follow gurus or mystics or psychics, there is the idea that all this learning and enlightenment is to make us better people.

But what do you understand by 'better'? More good? Less judgmental and superficial? More charitable? In Darwinian terms, a 'better' person would be one best suited to its environment; in other words, one who can outrun and outswim predators, doesn't need shelter from the elements, and doesn't have to expend energy to get food. So by that definition we're all absolutely dreadful people. Or is our environment the concrete jungle? If that's the case, is a 'better' person one who has a car, a house, a steady income, doesn't take risks, and aspires to having children who will in turn gain similar possessions and values? Aren't we heading back towards mediocrity again? It's all so vague, and vague goals are bad goals.

However, the main problem with believing that the purpose of life is to become a nice person is that it undermines the value of intelligence. It's all around us all the time in Western culture, on television and newspapers and greeting cards: it's okay if you don't know anything about anything, as long as you're a sweet person and you phone your mom on Mother's Day.

You have to be a serious meathead to believe that. And yet who can blame the average person, when they're being exposed not only to the constant glorification of emotion over intellect, but they're actually being encouraged to be suspicious of science and reason. Just think about how often kid's television pro-grammes feature a bad guy who speaks well (usually with an English accent, if the show is American), who is a scientist, and who is very intelligent. Think of how many pop songs urge us to 'follow our hearts' over our minds. I'm sorry, but we've been there and we've done that, and the result was witch-burning, supersti-tion, tribal warfare and genocide.

Somehow mediocrity has hijacked us, and is urging us and our children to reject intellectual development as somehow cold and scheming. But we are meant to improve our minds. We're here to learn. Feeling is secondary, and often leads us down the wrong path. I get very frustrated with pop-psychologists and feel-good counsellors who tell people that we're here to learn how to love. Please! This is the worst possible place to learn how to love. It's an ideal training ground to learn how to hate, resent, envy and mock, but that's about all.

We're losing our God-given ability to question, to doubt and to debate. Perhaps it's all part of the 'dumbing down' of Western culture, a process accelerated by greedy industries that want us to stop thinking so we'll buy more. But whatever its cause, it separates us further from God. Because we're not encouraged to challenge or argue or question, we start accepting things on faith alone, and that includes God. In the ultimate irony, God has become a holy cow!

When you were a teenager, didn't you question your parents? Didn't you yell and scream at them, accusing them of being unfair and mean and heartless? Well then, why don't you feel comfortable yelling and screaming at God? Are you afraid He's going to smite you with a thunderbolt or turn you into a pillar of salt? Your parents didn't do that, so why should God?

I fight with God all the time. And like a good parent, He doesn't fight back. He just waits until I'm done and then, one day, I realize that maybe I wasn't totally in the right, that maybe I didn't quite understand the situation as well as I thought I did.

Phoning home

This is a short chapter, but a very important one, and one that I hope will answer a question you might have been asking while reading this book, or had thought of before you even found this book.

As you now know, we are extremely busy in the Hereafter. Yes, we rest initially, but soon we plunge into a welter of discovery and hard work, analysing, reflecting, making huge and difficult decisions about our fates and the paths we want to follow. Then we're either setting off into a new universe of knowledge and experience, or returning through the veil of forgetfulness to reincarnate into this concrete world to undergo new experiences or to process unfinished business. It all seems very hectic, and very focused.

So why, in all this activity, would the dead want to talk to us here in this world? Why would they bother, when where they find themselves is so much more important and demanding? Surely 'phoning home', through mediums or in visions or dreams, is the last thing on their list of priorities?

But the simple answer is that spirits do regularly want to get in contact with us, and they have their own very compelling reasons for doing so.

A common reason for trying to send a cross-dimensional message is if justice hasn't been done. In extreme cases, this means a murderer has gone free, or a treacherous family member has got away with some sort of huge injustice, be it fraud or incest. But of course there are other failures of justice: a deceased father sees that his children are being ill-treated by a step-father, or an inheritance is being abused by surviving family members.

Sometimes those on the first level after this world discover that they have things they need to teach us. It could be that they have found a calling to be spirit guides (see the next chapter), but there doesn't have to be anything ordained or vocational about the desire to teach: we all want to teach and enlighten those we love, or those who have the potential to harm those we love.

Spirits also contact us in an attempt to protect us: they might have learned something in the Hereafter, heard about a potential threat on the heavenly grapevine. The first inkling of a preventable fatal disease, an abusive spouse, a disastrous career decision: all can prompt a call from the afterlife. Remember, just because those on the other side are involved in a complex and demanding new life, it does not mean they have forgotten us or love us any less. The desire to rush to the aid of our family, to save them from danger, remains just as strong in the Hereafter.

However, souls are not always allowed to do this, and usually first have to find out whether or not they are permitted to dabble in earthly affairs in this way. This is because those on the other side are absolutely forbidden to interfere with our free will. There are very strict rules about this, and a soul that sneaks across with information that we in this life should not have access to, is risking very bad karma.

But perhaps the main reason the dead want to contact those

they leave behind is to give them proof of survival. And I have to tell you that this isn't out of any noble or altruistic desire on the part of the dead: they basically want to shut us up! Our outpouring of grief upsets them (we all hate seeing our loved ones suffer or grieve), but instead of being able to shut a door or put down a phone, they feel and hear that grief all the time. They appreciate it at first, certainly, but their new life is so dynamic, and their experiences so vivid, that this thin, dark wail from our slow, dull world begins to grate, like the sound of a crying baby in an airliner. It sounds rather callous, but they contact us to give us closure, so that we'll stop bugging them and they can get on with doing what they have to do! The dead have better things to do than to come and hold our hands.

You'd assume that it's much harder for the living to contact the dead than vice versa, but you'd be wrong: getting a message through to earth from the Hereafter is not a simple matter. They can't just close their eyes, click their heels together and say, 'There's no place like home!' to get an instant connection into our minds. Likewise they can't always manifest as people or ghosts in this world, and often they don't want to: if you wanted to get a message across, appearing as a ghost might be an absolute disaster, since the message would be lost amid the general shrieking and diving out of windows that would no doubt ensue.

So they do what we do in life when we can't go direct: they use a middleman. Enter the common or garden psychic. But even this process isn't as easy for them as you'd assume. Despite having access to enormous amounts of information on the other side, most of the spirits who have come to me, asking me to pass on messages, found me through referrals! I've discovered it works along very similar lines to finding a good doctor in this world. You don't look through the Yellow Pages: you ask around. And since there aren't many genuine or good mediums in the world, more often than not they come to see me, or the other well-known international psychics.

It's quite a literal process. I live in Cape Town, South Africa, so those who want to contact people here have to ask around for a medium in South Africa! And I can tell you that they do shop around: spirits don't have some God-given higher knowledge about the quality of mediums. In fact it's not unusual for them to approach a medium and to leave disappointed.

So that's one half of the conversation taken care of, but it's no use phoning if there's no-one at home to answer. Often spirits need to pull some strings on the other side to get us in the right place to hear them. Obviously they can't move us physically, or override our brains and steer us like little zombies to the nearest psychic, but they find other ways.

For example, I did a live stage show for some weeks in 2003, and we had advertising posters on most of Cape Town's highways. During the show's run a woman came to me and said she'd been driving home one day, and had glanced up and seen one of the posters. She was an entirely ordinary person, not one swayed by advertising or spiritual mumbo-jumbo. She had no demons of remorse or guilt overpowering her senses. She was not needy or empty. And yet as she looked briefly at the poster she heard a voice. She knew the voice: it belonged to someone who'd died years ago, whom she hadn't thought of for years. And it was telling her, 'Go! Go!'

Now this is a fairly dramatic and obvious example, and you might say that it was a blessing she didn't freak out and wrap her car around a lamp-post, as someone with more fragile nerves might have done. But it worked, and she came to see me, and I passed on the messages she needed to hear.

Sometimes when my life intersects with someone who has a message waiting for them, it all seems like a huge and very far-fetched coincidence. But mostly there's nothing coincidental about it. It's all just very long-range logistics and planning working out. For example, if you didn't know how air travel and airports worked, you might think that it's an amazing coincidence that you arrive in London just before another flight is leaving for New York, and that not only is there a space on that flight, but it's booked in your name. But we understand cause and effect in this world, with its laws of physics and statistical likelihood and all those things that govern us, and so flying to New York seems predictable and not at all mysterious or paranormal.

Some years ago a man from Pretoria came to me for a session. We were going along as normal, until suddenly I had to stop.

'I'm sorry,' I said, 'but we've got company.' There was a little girl in the room. 'She says her name is Clare[1], and she's calling to you.'

'To me?'

'She's desperate to get in touch with her parents,' I explained to him. 'She's calling you uncle.'

And of course what emerged was typical. She had known this man while she was alive in this world, and had come to him to get in touch with her parents. She had not been able to go straight to them. Grief is like a veil that is drawn down over people, making them blind and deaf to everything except their suffering. Little Clare had come up against that veil: you can't reach those who can't see. It took the 'coincidental' intervention of someone less affected by the death of the little girl to lift that veil. I am confident that she guided the man to me, whether it was by discreet nudging ('I wonder what it would be like to see a psychic?') or by more aggressive urging ('I wonder what's happened to poor little Clare?').

---

[1] This is not the name the child told me: I must respect my clients' confidentiality, and also that of those who contact them.

Another example of this cropped up at one of my regular larger readings at a hotel in Cape Town. The room was packed, people were asking me things left and right, and there were spirits pouring in, all wanting to be heard. But there was a woman standing at the back of the crowd who hadn't said anything or asked anything. And between her and me was the spirit of a man, who was clearly there to contact her.

I stopped and told the woman that I needed to address this spirit, and he told me that he was her father, who had died when she was just four years old. He told me that they had never spoken or communicated since his death, and she confirmed that this was the case. So here he was, standing patiently and quietly in this busy forum, waiting his turn. And what was his message? It was simple and beautiful. He just wanted to say hello to his child. That was all, and then he left.

On a lighter note I have to address another question of 'phoning home' that skeptics always tease me about. In fact I'm sure you've also watched psychics on the telly and wondered the same thing. If those on the other side are suddenly more advanced than we are, and if the next level is one where information and communication are no longer restricted by physical things like books and wires and sounds and words, why are the messages from the other side so often garbled or fragmented? Why do the spirits suddenly seem to lose the ability to construct complete sentences, and insist on communicating by murmuring, 'Blue socks! Blue socks!' or repeating nonsensical phrases about Aunt Milly and egg-beaters and catnip?

I mean, we've all seen the television psychics clutching their ears dramatically, with eyes squeezed tight shut, saying, 'I'm getting something … it's a … it's an ear-bud. What meaning does an ear-bud have to you, Tammy-Fay?' It seems phony, but I must stress that this technique reflects what I myself experience. The reason so many messages seem disjointed or garbled is that it's often very difficult to hear what is being said. The only thing I can compare it to is listening to someone speaking underwater. Some words are clear, but the rest is just a wowing, bubbling sound.

Considering all the talk that happens in my average session with a client (me blabbing away, them umming and ahing or adding bits here and there), it can be a real strain trying to listen to three spirits as well, all of them talking at once. I'll be the first to acknowledge that this bad connection makes us look like fakes: 'Uncle Jim! No? Uncle James? Oh, *under* James!' At this point it looks like I'm just making stuff up!

It can often become overwhelming. Years ago I lived around the corner from a very large cemetery. Big mistake. It was like trying to sleep in a bus station. The spirits of the recently dead would troop in and out, all clamoring for my attention and my services, wanting to get the message back to their families that they were alright. It was just crazy.

South Africa is by international standards a fairly religious country. But somehow I'd managed to land up in the middle of Atheistville! The vast majority of these souls hadn't believed in life after death before their own deaths, and presumably they'd left behind families with similar beliefs, so of course they were quite desperate to get the good news across.

But where the recently departed are concerned, you're dealing with a real stampede. Before they've understood their new state, or come to terms with their deaths, they are still fairly disoriented and skittish. Psychic ability in the earthly world shines out like a beam of light through the confusion, and they are instinctively drawn to that light. But of course they don't really know what they're doing, and they are often very inappropriate and clumsy. They haven't figured out the protocol yet!

I had to lay down the law with those spirits, and it still sometimes happens today. I'll wake up and there'll be a mournful-looking spirit, a little apologetic, who wants to tell me something. I can really lose my cool at these moments, but mostly I bite my lip and say, 'Look, it's after hours, I'm not in spirit yet, I'm trying to catch up on my beauty rest, and you really need to leave now!'

Most of them slink off sheepishly, especially when I use my physical voice to underline my point. They can obviously read my thoughts, but hearing those thoughts expressed in actual sound – and often quite loudly! – gives them a little kick in the pants.

Guides, angels and other light beings

A guided tour

Maybe it's because there are so many psychics on television these days. Maybe more people are spending their lunch-breaks in bookshops skimming through esoteric or mystical books. Maybe it's just a comforting idea that is easy to latch on to. But whatever the case, everybody seems to know about guides nowadays.

I don't want to say it's much ado about nothing, because guides are important and are doing the best they can; but there are considerably more important aspects to the Hereafter that people would do better to focus on, rather than obsessing about whether or not they have a guide, and who and what it is. In fact it sometimes seems that, as far as the public is concerned, guides are the rock stars of the Hereafter. And as usual they ignore the song writer: in this case, God.

But just in case you've missed out on all the hype, a short explanation is in order.

Guides are simply souls on the next level, the first level of heaven, who act as counsellors and, well, guides, to us on earth. They are not angels, or archangels, or light beings, or a specific 'soul group', as some people claim. Neither are they a spiritual task-force, a kind of specially organized heavenly SWAT team trained by God to keep bogeys off our backs. They are souls like you and me, who, for whatever reason, are now helping us poor clumsy mortals down here.

We don't all have guides, for the simple reason that we don't all need guides. In this world many businessmen and politicians have advisors. But the vast majority of people get by without professional or specialist advice, usually relying on their own instincts or the advice of people they trust. If you don't need an advisor, you might not need a guide.

On the other hand, you could argue that people without a human advisor are probably making very good use of their guide! But I bring this up simply to underline the fact that our relationship with the guides on the other side is not an eternal constant, in the way that our relationship with our guardian angel is. I'll discuss guardian angels in more detail shortly.

So who are the guides, and why do they do what they do?

In the chapter about the Halls of Learning I discussed the issue of our responsibility to others. We have a duty to share our talents and gifts with those around us, and guides have reached a point in their evolution where they are ideally suited to helping us down here. But they aren't freelance altruists or do-gooders. You can't decide to become a guide and then gallop off on your own crusade. Guides are appointed. Of course they have the right to turn down the offer: it isn't something we all have to do as part of our learning process, and no soul can be forced to help another. But generally they are in a state in which guiding seems the next logical step, and they seldom do turn down the offer.

This all sounds rather mystical, if not a little over-complicated, but the requirements for being a guide are no different to those qualities we look for in this world when we're searching for advice: expertise in a particular field, and experience. Lots of experience.

Bear in mind that guides are simply souls on the next level, and no more advanced or angelic than any one of us, so of course their expertise is going to be fairly specialized. We all learn many different skills over the course of our lifetimes, but it's very rare that a soul masters a wide range of disciplines. For instance someone with a talent for music would rediscover that talent in life after life, and develop it further. It's very unlikely that a soul would be a composer in one life, a mechanic in the next and a businessman in the next.

Even someone like Leonardo da Vinci, whom we remember and admire as a 'Renaissance Man' – someone blessed with an apparently enormous range of talents – was limited in some ways. He wrote no music, made no medical discoveries, was an ordinary businessman, and practised a very orthodox brand of religion.

But of course most of us would give our back teeth to have someone like Leonardo as our guide, which simply underlines the fact that we don't want or need guides with a wide spread of gifts.

What we do need, however, is experience. The most important requirement for becoming a guide is a long history of reincarnation. I can't emphasise this enough. Guides need to have been around the block so many times that they've worn a groove in the pavement. They must know humanity as well as a favourite old jersey, every crinkle and crease and moth-hole. After all, they're going to be helping us with very human problems: troubles with money, with love, with growing up or growing old. As Steve Martin's snake-oil charlatan faith healer says in his final confession in *Leap of Faith*, 'If you want to know about sin, who're you going to ask? Some virgin priest or a sinner?' Our world is no place for helpful theories about existence from other-worldly bystanders: we need practical advice from people who've been there, done that, got the T-shirt and worn holes in it!

It is tempting to think of guides as the personal trainers of the Hereafter, gurus who have access to the Akashic Record and can slip us some answers through the back door between worlds. But in truth they have very little autonomy. Remember, they are appointed, which implies control from higher up the chain. They are given assignments, and are briefed and debriefed just like any consultant or hired advisor. In other words, while they draw on their own knowledge and expertise, they very seldom use their own initiative.

The reason for this lack of creativity on their part is straight-forward. Think in terms of an advisor in this world: if you had an advisor, a guide, whom you believed to be enormously gifted and insightful, and they used their initiative and began suggest-ing all kinds of courses of action for you to take, or began nudg-ing you in this direction or that, what would you do? You bet you'd do exactly what they said! That's just common sense.

But guides – and in fact all other higher beings – are strictly forbidden from interfering with our free will. No light being, angel or even archangel, is permitted to get in the way of our decisions, or influence them unduly. Offering us advice unasked, or showing us possibilities that we haven't thought of ourselves, would almost certainly hamper that freedom of choice, since we'd feel compelled by their otherworldly insight to obey them.

If you take one thing away from this chapter, it should be the recognition that guides are a great boon in our lives, that the information at their disposal is extraordinary, and that their experience enables them to give us valuable advice about most things we ask them; but that they are not essential. And more importantly: their advice isn't always what we should follow.

Remember, guides are still involved in their own develop-ment. They haven't reached any destination yet. Yes, they've lived many lives and experienced far more than most of us have, but that doesn't necessarily mean they've mastered anything.

Remember the old souls? It's not quite the same as being 25 in Matric, but experience doesn't always equal wisdom.

When I was still channelling guides (read on to find out why I stopped!), I got to know one Brother John, who had been hanged, drawn and quartered and stuck on a gate in China, which is really enough to ruin your whole day. Brother John brought through some astonishing information that helped change someone's life in this world, but despite this he was still fairly ordinary and not a highly evolved being.

Of course the most important fact about the advice of guides is this: they are still learning. And what is the best way to learn? All right, we've already said that experience is a priceless learning tool. But what *specific* aspect of experience do we learn most from? Think about your own career and the moments in which you made little leaps ahead, changed gears. Were they moments where everything was going smoothly, or were they days on which you'd made a horrible mistake, and had a strip torn off you?

Whether we're children touching a hot stove or adults investing in a pyramid scheme, our learning process is accelerated by one common denominator: mistakes. We learn by making mistakes, by going down one path and finding a dead end, and then retracing our steps and making a better decision.

So if the guides are still learning, by definition they're making plenty of mistakes. And a lot of those are at our expense. Let's pretend you've asked your guide, through quiet meditation, whether you need to start your own business. You've got two ideas: you could either open a chicken farm, or sell barbed wire to chicken farmers. You open your inner ear, the ear of the subconscious through which guides speak to us, and listen …

The answer comes quickly. Chicken farming is splendid. Farm chickens. Chickens are your future.

Now of course he would say that, because he was a chicken

farmer 1000 years ago and he found inner peace among the chooks in his yard, so he thinks you'd find similar benefits. But he hasn't noticed that you live in Jackal Valley, and within a week your chickens are just a few feathers fluttering on the fence.

Your guide has a big think: what went wrong? What mistakes did I make here? Oh, he says, now I see – jackal, sharp teeth, chicken, soft neck. Bingo! Another piece of enlightenment for your guide, a big fat failure for you.

Remember: *Guides know more than us, but they can be wrong. Only God can never be wrong.*

Luckily guides are often enlightened enough to know their own limitations. Sometimes if they don't know an answer, or aren't qualified to address your concerns, they will introduce another guide and step back. Which of course dismisses the theory that we have one guide allocated to us, who stays with us for our whole lives. This is just not true. The only otherworldly constant in our lives on this planet are our guardian angels, but I'm getting ahead of myself again.

It's quite a romantic concept, this notion of a special confidant and advisor shepherding us through the trials of life. It's not surprising that people have built them up into something they're not. And it's also not surprising that guides are believed to be essential and all-knowing. I've encountered workshops and so-called teaching circles where people meet to wax lyrical about guides, almost entirely ignoring God, and, more sinisterly, where the advice from the other side is held up like some sort of gospel or revelation.

When you ask your best friends for advice, do you always accept what they say? Of course you don't. Sometimes you simply thank them, and ditch their advice on the spot. So why would you cling to advice from someone you don't love or respect, in fact someone you've never even met? Yes, they have access to the Akashic Record, but we all do, given the right training and meditation. It's time for people to stop mistaking the training wheels for the entire bicycle!

I know this all sounds as if I'm knocking guides. I'm not. They do a great deal of good. But I want to demystify them a little. Personally I wouldn't want to be a guide, and so far I haven't been one. I think the aspect I'd hate most is the meetings. Yes, like all good appointees, they meet regularly to discuss interesting cases, ask each other advice, maybe swap clients! But we all know what goes on in business meetings: endless talk, resulting in, well, the decision to talk further about possible actions …

Channel surfing

Contacting your guide is relatively easy. You don't need to come to me for a description and point-by-point biography. Besides, you'd probably be disappointed since most guides were just ordinary folks in past lives, Ukrainian nuns or German farmers or Ethiopian scholars. If you were hoping you had Moses or Cleopatra or Albert Einstein peering over your shoulder, I'm afraid I'm going to rain on your parade …

In fact, put all that noise and hype out of your head. Guides are not accessories or status symbols. These are earthly concerns that will get in the way of hearing the advice you are offered. Just concentrate on the problem before you. Perhaps you are torn between two choices. Perhaps you feel snarled up in a huge tangle of confusion and powerlessness. Picture your problem, feel it and acknowledge it. Even think of certain scenes, concrete examples that have upset or confused you: an argument with someone in a busy street, a moment of despair at work or on the bus, the faces of the people you have to choose between or bring together.

And now just ask. Without vanity or pretence, simply present the problem to whomever you feel is listening, whether that is a guide, your guardian angel, or even God. Lay all your cards on the table, and then walk away.

But in the minutes and hours and days that follow, listen. I don't mean that you should sit still and strain to hear something. You'll probably only hear your heart pounding as you drive your blood pressure through the roof from all the strain. Just be aware that you have cast a line out into the great lake of the universe, your question bobbing there like a trout-fly, and as you go about your business, keep a soft touch on the that line. Check in with your question every so often. Be aware of new whispers in your subconscious. Listen to the strange little phrases that pop into your head while you're on the treadmill at the gym.

Because at some stage that line will twitch, and your question will be addressed. Perhaps it won't be answered, but perhaps that will be an answer in itself. But whatever you hear, be it in a particularly striking dream or in a strangely affecting conversation with a friend at work, be ready to listen and to acknowledge that you have been heard.

A twitch of a line? A vague sense of being heard? An answer so subtle it might be confused for a change of mood or the rumbling of an empty stomach? To a modern Westerner, this is a desperately unsatisfying state of affairs! Raised in a culture that becomes bored with any experience not publicized in five-metre high neon or accompanied by a star-studded rock opera, many people reject the secret and subtle processes of the inner ear. Like hyperactive children we fidget and pout, and the answers escape us.

Enter channelling, the Las Vegas of the psychic world, its messages as clear and glamorous as a neon billboard. But like the hedonist's paradise in Nevada, the glow and glitz often hide sinister forces at work beyond the glare of the lights. Most visitors see a great show, catch a thrill here and there, and leave with a smile. A few – the ones you never hear about – retreat back to their lives ruined and disturbed, destined for a life of regret.

In a nutshell, channelling sees a psychic or mystic using their own body as a conduit for spirits who want to get messages across. This is not possession: the spirit has not taken over the psychic's body, but is rather only using its various tools – voice, hands, facial features – to communicate to the living on this side.

Nevertheless, it is a dangerous and extremely traumatic process for whoever is doing the channelling. On the few occasions I have done it, I have been gripped by extreme nausea, pain and disorientation, and the state I've entered has been very similar to an epileptic seizure or trance. My conventional clairvoyant work does not demand that I push myself so close to the edge of what I can handle, since I can enter the necessary trance-like state as easily as turning on a switch. All the same, if I do too many readings in a single day I feel drained and fairly nauseous.

And yet even standard channelling is relatively safe when compared with voice channelling – where the spirit's actual voice comes out of the medium's mouth – and transfigurations. This final practice is genuinely frightening for those unused to the quirks of the Hereafter, because the face of the psychic or medium slowly begins to alter until it transfigures into the face of the spirit who is being channelled. As you can imagine, it is extremely stressful, both physically and emotionally, and people have died performing these rituals.

But still people want the instant solution, the dramatic revelation, and so channelling becomes ever more popular and widely practised. And as the boundaries blur between meditation and entertainment, so more and more mediums are channelling guides. I've been pretty emphatic about some of my beliefs so far in this book, but one of my strongest is about the danger and disrespect inherent in messing around with forces that we are not strong enough to control, or else too weak to do without once we've started.

Let me be very clear on this: guides are not our buddies, and more importantly, they are not our servants. They are not there to be summoned into our world to sort out our incompetence and weakness. I am infuriated when I hear about alternative healers or practitioners of psychic surgery channelling guides who then perform the healing. This is an abomination and fla-grant abuse of the resources of the Hereafter. Contact with guides, in fact with all things that lie beyond death, is supposed to empower us, not encourage us to stand back and let Dr Ching from the first Ming Dynasty do the dirty work for us.

It's not surprising then, given the fact that so many people exploring the esoteric world are bone idle and naïve, that the channelling of guides can become an addiction or a crutch. In my introduction I mentioned that there are people in the world who are joiners and workshop junkies, who need every answer or instruction handed to them wrapped in cottonwool or coated in honey. They are helpless in every sense, and have surrendered all responsibility for their lives to others. Every so often I will expe-rience this too, when a person becomes addicted to readings. When it happens I cut them off, cold turkey, so that they will have a chance to rediscover their own wills and motives.

Well you can just imagine the appeal of honest-to-goodness guides to this kind of person. After all, if they'll beat down my door for another smidgen of insight, just think of how they yearn for a source closer to the truth, closer to God.

Of course, the guides aren't helpless bystanders in all of this. Perhaps I've painted a picture to suggest that as soon as they are channelled, they are sucked down a sort of trans-dimensional drainpipe into a human medium; but this isn't the case at all. They allow themselves to be channelled, because they want to serve and help, and often consider this an excellent opportunity to have their advice heard by people who might otherwise over-look the more subtle messages coming across.

And the guides know an unhealthy situation when they see one. I have known them to withdraw as soon as they've realized that people are becoming dependent on them. Of course when they do retreat the person they've left is as traumatized and enraged as any addict deprived of a fix, even more so if they feel that God has turned His back on them by withholding His helpers or favours. But usually this trauma is, in Shakespeare's words, full of sound and fury, signifying nothing.

Guides know an unhealthy situation when they see one, but what happens when they can't see one? I've explained how, in many ways, guides are not very much more enlightened than we are, and we are often ridiculously blind to our own failings and defects. How often obsessions or compulsions or delusions creep up on us, and when they're finally revealed by a friend or therapist or minister, we are flabbergasted that we didn't see them coming. Guides are no safer from these all-too-human problems. They might have an enormous amount of experience, but experience doesn't always translate into insight.

The reality is that there are guides – not many, but enough to make this a real concern – who reverse the conventional obsession, and become too dependent on the person they're guiding at that point. You can just imagine what a nest of vipers this little duo becomes, a mutually parasitic relationship that makes Macbeth and his lady look like babes in the wood!

These are guides who have been sidetracked. They've enjoyed their role for so long that they've forgotten why they started doing it. And to a certain extent they've become addicted to the endless variety in the lives they're observing. We're quite a soap opera down here, and in a way it's understandable that souls who enjoy being involved in the day-to-day doings of others might become sucked in by all the melodrama and intrigue. If you've ever watched the soaps, you'll know what I'm talking about. Watch one, and you laugh dismissively and shake your head at the stupidity of people who rush home to watch every day. Watch two, and suddenly you're aware that Clancy and

DeShawn aren't actually the parents of little Lulu-May, and suddenly it doesn't seem quite so stupid any more. Watch three or five, and you don't know what you ever did in the afternoons before you discovered all this! Obviously it's dangerous and unhelpful for guides to become addicted, but I can't pretend not to understand the appeal.

Pushing the limits
When you think of channelling, you probably imagine the psychic as some kind of conduit, a sort of spiritual hosepipe, and while most mediums probably wouldn't be thrilled at being compared to garden equipment, the analogy is pretty accurate.

But I've been speaking about the dangers of channelling, and perhaps you've had a harder time imagining why this might be dangerous. Sure, you can understand the nausea and the headaches (after all, most people get these just by watching half an hour of children's cartoons in the morning!), but why should it be so dangerous? The spirit isn't possessing the medium, and since there's no physical interaction between the two, why should the medium be in physical danger? Surely the 'hosepipe' stays unharmed as the 'water' flows through it?

Mostly, but not always. Guides are impressive souls. They are filled with knowledge, glowing with energy and life. They have instant access to large sections of the Akashic Record (or at least those sections they are permitted to absorb). In short, this isn't Great Aunt Bessy wanting to be channelled so she can remind her surviving family to add chunks to the cat's meat and to put her knitting in mothballs. These are weighty spirits, chosen to be guides because of their experience and their sense of duty and responsibility.

So if Aunt Bessy is 'water' in the 'hosepipe', how could we describe a guide as it comes through the medium? Simple. It's a deluge. It's a dam bursting through a single sluice. The pressure is immense, and sometimes that thin little hosepipe, this frail little mind and body that we have, simply gives way.

Still, it's possible to channel guides and get away relatively unscathed. But I believe that it is entirely impossible for a human being to channel anything higher or more advanced. I know a very sweet man who does good work in our field, who insists that he channels angels. Now I'm sorry, but if a human channelled an angel, that human would leave this mortal coil in the most sudden and spectacular style! I don't know if he'd physically explode or catch fire, or just fall over in a heap, but either way he'd be toast.

But that doesn't stop people from trying. There are an awful lot of spirit beings out in the universe, some benevolent, some demonic, some confused, and some that are just plain confusing; and people being what they are, it's a safe bet that psychics around the world have tried channelling at least a small part of this spiritual zoo. There's a famous psychic in the United States who channels someone called Ramtha. I know Ramtha sounds like a treatment for athlete's foot, but apparently he's a 35,000-year-old warrior who appeared in her kitchen in 1977. To find out more, go to one of her seminars. If you can spare the $1000 …

Angels

Angels are not metaphors. They are not analogies. Likewise they are not chubby-cheeked white children from the American Midwest playing harps and singing incessantly. Angels are real. Angels are eternal. Like tuning forks they resound with the beauty of God's creation. Like pure crystal they catch His light and cast it elsewhere. They are empty and they are full. They are kind and they are cruel. They are what they are, and they are what God intended for them to be. Understand this, and allow yourself to accept it for a moment.

The last decade has seen an amazing surge of interest in angels, from Oprah publicizing her 'Angel Network' to Emma Thompson hamming it up in a pair of beautiful white wings in *Angels in America*. And frankly, it's about time. Angels inspire awe and wonder and joy, just as they demand respect and sometimes fear. They are magnificent, titanic servants of God, and at their head stand the archangels, the iconic and original children of God, each one an astonishing creature and entirely unique from the others.

Of all the topics covered in this book, angels deserve their own volume. They are too complex, demand too much awe and honour, to be glossed over in a few short pages; and so what follows is really just a sketch of the angelic host. This is not a compressed course in angelology, because that would be a contradiction in terms. But it is important to understand, however superficially, the relationship we have with angels, and specifically our guardian angel. And I think it's also important to explain the roles of guardian angels versus those of guides. After all, why even have guides if we have guardian angels, who are so much more powerful and wise?

It's a fair question, and this whole question of jurisdiction – which seems to have the potential to turn into a kind of benevolent spiritual turf-war! – is not something people often think about, even those who believe in both guides and guardian angels.

For starters, though, let me make one thing crystal clear. There is simply no comparison between guides and guardian angels when it comes to authority. There isn't a turf-war or a tug-of-war over who gets to look after us, simply because angels are beyond even the wildest imaginings of guides (who are just souls on the next level). I've said that you should be comfortable with rejecting or ignoring advice from your guides, but when an angel tells you to jump, you ask how high.

But of course the difference between guides and guardian

angels is obvious if you just stop and think about their names. Guides guide us, guardian angels guard us: it's that simple.

And now we get to the really fascinating part, where our human assumptions about greatness and power have to be rearranged. Archangels have free will, as we know all too well from the myth of the fallen angels; but the host below them, including our guardian angels, *do not have free will.* They are pure and awesome (in the true sense of the word), and yet we puny little scraps of life down on this wretched, violent world have more freedom than they do.

We are raised to treasure free will, to regard it as one of the most essential aspects of being a valuable human being. We are urged to pity those nameless, anonymous drones we see in footage of Communist China under Mao, or of enormous stadiums in North Korea full of chanting, apparently mindless people stripped of their free will. We shiver slightly when we think of a future in which robots will have not only intelligence, but free will: only people, we assume, and only good insightful people, should have free will.

I believe that free will is desperately important to our species, but that doesn't mean that I consider it universally necessary. In fact you only have to look around you to see that free will is the exception rather than the rule. Bees perform their roles apparently without choosing to. Even our beloved pets, those cats and dogs that we've imbued with so many human characteristics, are slaves to their instincts and stomachs.

In other words, accept that guardian angels are no less angelic because they don't make conscious decisions about their actions. Like bees, or the great flocks of swallows that navigate the globe, or any of the millions of species that surge around this planet all the time, all busily living and dying by rules not of their making, angels are fulfilling their role in the universe, the role they were designed to fulfil.

That role is guardianship. If guides are our advisors, then guardian angels are our bodyguards, appointed to watch over us from the moment of our birth. Again, this isn't a metaphorical or figurative kind of protection. Some years ago I was on a bus, standing near the door, when suddenly I was physically picked up and flung off into the street. Seconds later a huge explosion tore through the bus, killing dozens of passengers. I don't know why there was a bomb on the bus, or why the other passengers weren't saved, but I do know that my guardian angel saved my life.

Archangels

I like the Archangels. It sounds a flippant thing to say, but I do. There are some, though, that I'm not crazy about, but now isn't the time or place to go into all of that. Besides, I've already been struck by lightning once! There we were, my daughter and I, sitting under a tree on a perfect day. Just one little cloud in the sky, far away. And next thing – crack, bang, fizz, the tree was toast. I was literally buzzing for the rest of the day: thunderstorms heighten my clairvoyant senses drastically, so you can just imagine how I was staggering about pretty wide-eyed.

Of course I'm joking about being zapped by archangels: they've got better things to do than police their egos. But they are complex, ancient, and, in limited human terms, morally ambiguous in a way that demands a cautious approach.

For instance, archangels make mistakes.

This is going to get me stoned next time I go to the marketplace! First I say angels are automata, now I say archangels are fallible. What next? God is a woman? Well, you'll just have to get to the chapter about Kabbalah to light that particular firecracker!

But it's true: archangels can make mistakes, for the simple reason that they have free will. Anything able to make its own decisions will, by definition, mess up now and then. From Eve's decision to taste the apple of Knowledge through to all those who didn't buy shares in a little company called Microsoft, our species is defined by its freedom to sail up the creek without the paddle. And we share this trait with the archangels.

Is it contradictory to say that the lesser angels are infallible simply because they're limited? I don't think so. Bees don't go wrong. Birds don't regularly get lost or stage riots come migration time.

But archangels can go wrong, and they already have. The revolution in heaven, the pride and creative obsession of Lucifer and his rebel angels, their attempts to create an earthly paradise in which they would be worshipped: all were big, big mistakes.

The Bible's angels

For many agnostics and atheists, the Bible's account of the archangel Gabriel is simply a parable, like so many others in the holy text. It's a story that is easily rationalized. For instance, the ancients interpreted everything and anything as a sign of God, so perhaps Mary was mistaking some morning sickness for a divine visitation. Or she dreamt it. Or it was a magnificent excuse to explain how an unwed girl, apparently a virgin, could get pregnant.

But these are limited views that deny the realities of Jesus of Nazareth, that he was a prophet and sage blessed with heavenly insights that had the power to save humanity from itself.

So assuming that Mary was visited by a being from somewhere other than the earthly plane, what was this being? Was the mother of Christ visited by one of the most powerful entities in the universe, namely the archangel Gabriel, or was it her guide manifesting as a visible light? Or was it her grandmother appearing to her?

I believe that it was Gabriel. In the original Hebrew the name of Gabriel contains the word 'Gav' which means 'the back (of God)', but it also contains the word 'Gevver', which means 'man'. It seems very fitting that the birth of Christ should have been heralded by an angel called, roughly translated, 'the man standing behind God'. Of all the archangels it seems most likely that it would have been Gabriel entrusted with this task.

For Christians the birth of Christ forms the hinge of the universe, the focal point of life in this world and the next. But even if you don't believe the Christian doctrine, or don't believe that Jesus was the son of God, it's worth knowing one thing: archangels never appear on earth. They just don't come here. They can, but they don't. So for an archangel, and Gabriel no less, to come here and to appear to human eyes suggests that this was an immense moment in humanity's history and progression towards God.

I've also been asked about Moses' burning bush. Was God in the flames? Was it an angel manifesting as fire? I believe it was neither. God wasn't in the burning bush, because God can't be confined. Neither was it an angel, since the message seems to have come directly from God, unedited and unchannelled. The bush was real, and so was the fire that left the bush undamaged. It was that rarest of events – a confirmation of faith. A simple demonstration of something 'impossible', to be sure, but the ancients were simple people whose experience of the world was based on practical experience and common sense. There were myths and beliefs aplenty, but none of these had literal manifestation in daily life. To encounter a burning bush that was cool to the touch, while herding goats in the wilderness, would have been enough. What would it have taken today, in an era saturated with spectacular excess and ludicrous special effect and visual trickery?

Into the light

By now I hope you will have a feeling for how dynamic, how full of light and energy and growth the universe beyond our worldly existence is. Whether it be the souls of our families, slowly finding their way in the next level; guides negotiating our two worlds; angels performing their allotted tasks with the predictability and brilliance of stars; or archangels occupying those dimensions that lie beyond even the most fertile human imagination, this is a creation populated with mysterious and wonderful entities.

But there is one more addition to this list that I haven't discussed yet, since these entities are perhaps the least satisfying to our human minds. And yet they are almost as closely related to us on this world as the spirits of our ancestors, or our guides, since they are what we, with a little luck and a great deal of hard work, will become in time.

To describe something as a 'light being' is immediately unsatisfying. It is an ephemeral term, and perhaps, if you like your words a little more punchy, it treads too close to those irritatingly vague and melodramatic phrases favoured by some esoteric writers. But it is a useful description in one respect, since it begins to uncover the essence of God, the stuff that forms the basis of the universe: light. Just as carbon is the building block of life on earth, so light is that essential element from which everything on every level in the universe springs.

It sounds peculiar, I know. Space is dark. Our universe is pitch black, and the tiny points of light it contains seem terribly small and insignificant. But seeing isn't believing, or knowing. The truth is seldom what is visible.

Light beings are not mysterious. They are just another phase of the very logical, very clearly defined process that is our evolution toward God. But because they have shed almost everything we recognize as human, they are difficult for us to engage with or imagine. It's difficult to be interested in something you can't picture, or to feel a spiritual connection with something that has no face, and does not smile or talk. It's rather like trying to be excited about a sunbeam coming through your window. You can see it, lighting the floor and setting the specks of dust in your room alight like little stars, but it's still just a sunbeam.

Nevertheless, becoming a light being is a stage that we must aim for. There will come a time when the cycle of reincarnations and field-trips in the Halls of Learning has to come to an end. There will be a moment when we are finally ready to shed those mortal concerns, those glitches and wrinkles of personality and persona, and move into a realm of pure thought and energy. And this is when we become light beings. Fairly crude ones, to be sure – in terms of our education towards God, the second level is still kindergarten! – but we've started a new form of existence that will hopefully end in reunification with the sun of all suns.

Science talks about phase changes – the way in which a substance like water changes from solid to liquid to gas – and perhaps this is a good analogy to keep in mind. We on earth are dense and slow-moving, unable to adapt quickly either physically or spiritually. We are the 'ice' of the universe, clunky and cold and very physical. But when we die we enter our 'water' phase, freed of restrictions like shape and solidity. We can fill differently shaped spaces, and can move freely from one space to another. What causes ice to melt? Well, heat, which is simply the process of agitating the water molecules. In other words, a higher vibration – literally – has been reached.

Ice can become water easily, but water can also freeze again. This reverse process is, of course, reincarnation. But when our time of reincarnating is finally over, we enter a new phase, and become 'steam'. We are still the same substance we have been all along, matter separate and independent from God, but now it is very difficult to return to our 'water' state, and almost impossible for us to become 'ice'. Light beings are this 'steam', with souls diffuse enough to mingle with other souls. Even spiritual space is no longer a restriction.

It is always difficult to avoid becoming too literal, but it's very difficult to describe these more ethereal beings without using concrete imagery. However, remember that this is merely an analogy. Light beings are not water or steam or anything else. The Holy Ghost of Christianity is not condensation. God is not a big rain cloud or a humid atmosphere.

To talk of light beings is to talk of the insubstantial. This is the nature of their essence. The worlds they begin to inhabit are entirely unlike anything we can imagine. To describe them is not only impossible, but redundant: light beings no longer see in a physical way because there is nothing to see. Certainly they can manifest or visit in the first level of the Hereafter, and when they do the souls there see them as we here might experience spirits or ghosts – their appearance in the retirement village definitely gets tongues wagging and refocuses everyone on their spiritual study programme. But they cannot be channelled, and no longer even have a spirit body. They move as light moves, and communicate mind to mind.

But these are not fey moonbeams flitting about in an abstract universe, a universe that, without the benefits of sight and sound and emotion, sounds frankly deathly dull. No, light beings are still very much with us in the next level, demonstrating their extraordinary power and skill as teachers. And it is they who offer hope to the wretched souls in the Grey Zones, revealing themselves to those who are ready to see: simply their presence in that grim astral world has the power to uplift souls, literally, back into the cycle of learning and reincarnation. And like all higher beings, they have absolutely no interest in coming to our seedy little world! I imagine they'd come if sent for, but then of course God would never send a light being when He could send an angel, so don't hold your breath …

> Guides and angels are magnificent and complex. They are both deeply satisfying to speculate about: angels fire our imaginations, and guides stroke our egos and titillate our earthly desires for power and knowledge. But neither should be worshipped or obsessed over. Always look first to your own desires and motives, and then to God.

The occult

Things that go bump in the night
Police Fear Occult Links in Murder Case! My Year of Occult Hell! Occultists Prey on Helpless Nuns in Small Seaside Village! Demon Occultists Broke My Glasses and Stole My Lunchbox!

Okay, so the last two might be tenuous, but these are the sorts of headlines we're assailed with every so often, especially on front pages more concerned with sales than accurate reporting. Sex and murder sell, but if you're the editor of a tabloid, there's nothing like a good occult scandal to get those tills ringing.

The international media have done ferocious damage to our language over the years. Terrorists have become 'insurgents' or even 'activists'. 'Stakeholders' have suddenly become people with vested interests, rather than what they used to be: objective outsiders who held the stake in contention, while other contenders battled it out. Nobody knows what 'parameter' and 'paradigm' mean, and still we use them left, right and centre!

But almost no other word has been through the mill of the gutter press and sloppy public usage like 'occult'. Mention the word and your audience backs away slightly, imagining Satan-worshippers in orgies of evil, chomping the heads off chickens and tossing black goats off stormy cliffs. But look it up in a dictionary, and the results are quite disappointing by comparison. Here's what my *Concise Oxford Dictionary* has to say: *Occult (1): Kept secret, esoteric; recondite, mysterious, beyond the range of ordinary knowledge; involving the supernatural, mystical, magical.* It seems a little thin on chicken abuse. Indeed, it could be a fairly satisfactory description of what goes on in most religious seminaries. And senior citizens would find it a perfect explanation for what goes on inside computers and cell phones!

In fact, this definition seems so strangely out of synch with the idea we have about what constitutes the occult, that we can only assume one of two things has happened. Either the *Concise Oxford Dictionary* has been infiltrated by Freemasons and Satanists intent on keeping the heat off their nefarious practices, or we've become prejudiced about the word, associated as it so often is with half-truths and misinformation. In other words, we are ignorant about what constitutes this nebulous thing we call 'the occult'. And ignorance is dangerous.

This chapter is not a defense of harmful practices. I do not endorse any belief that denies, defies or defiles God. But denial and outright condemnation of alternative religious practices – especially by conservative organized religion – have left too many places too dark for too long. This chapter is a chance to cast some light on those places, to correct some harmful misconceptions and prejudices. Most importantly, it is an affirmation of good's duty to face and stare down evil, wherever it crops up and in whatever form. But first there are some serious misconceptions to be dealt with …

Just because I'm paranoid, it doesn't mean they aren't out to get me!

Yes, I'm afraid it does. Paranoia, especially about political conspiracies, has become fashionable in our time, helped largely by Hollywood and American television identifying fresh insecurities to mine. From the *X-Files* to *The Matrix* trilogy, young people are encouraged to believe that the truth is being hidden from them by nasty men in black suits. Ordinary people like you and me, who one would think wouldn't have time to worry about international conspiracies, are suddenly becoming increasingly aware of these accusations and allegations. A climate of hysteria is building (fuelled by the media magnates who get rich off our agitation) in which people who used to just get on with their lives suddenly have an opinion about things they couldn't possibly know anything about. George Bush rigged the 2000 American election! The invasion of Iraq was all about oil! The Pentagon has evidence of aliens! It was an American cruise missile that hit the Pentagon on 9/11! Osama Bin Laden is living in captivity in Guantanamo Bay!

These are pet theories that make people angry, but there are more vague conspiracy theories in wide circulation that seem to make people genuinely frightened. Most of these revolve around secret societies, like the Illuminati, the Bilderberg Group and the Freemasons, and all say basically one thing: our lives are being controlled by a small group of extremely powerful and wealthy people, who are elusive, secretive and potentially very dangerous. The truth is out there, say X-Files fans. Big Brother is watching, warn freedom lobbyists. They know where you live, whisper the media.

And I say: *Big deal! Who cares?* When you stop and think about these theories, they all boil down to the kind of ignorance and isolation from which so many members of the global middle class suffer. We are educated, and yet we know nothing about the secrets and undercurrents of international diplomacy and trade, and even if we knew who to ask, they wouldn't tell us! We have some money, but not nearly enough to wield any real power, and usually we and our money are simply being used as tools to entrench the truly wealthy elite further. If you have a bank account, right now you are being used by someone you've never met to finance his or her personal ambitions.

So to start panicking about men in dark suits monitoring your every move is downright childish. Dozens of companies know where you live, what you like and what you earn, but do you worry about them? Your government keeps entire libraries of secrets from you, and yet you continue to vote. If you have a cell phone on you, you can be tracked to with a few metres, anywhere in the world, and yet do you go around worrying that you're being monitored?

I suppose it's human nature to worry about the wrong things. At present everyone is so terrified of nuclear terrorism or the spread of radical Islam or the imperial ambitions of the United States, they've forgotten to worry about their planet, dying under their feet. Every year in the Amazon rainforest an area the size of Belgium is slashed and burned, usually illegally, and yet when last did you read a headline or see a news insert from Brazil?

But it's also human nature to fear secrecy. Secrets are always kept by a small elite, from which the rest of us are, by definition, excluded. Remember when you were seven or eight, and the other children kept secrets from you? Remember how upset it made you, even though you yourself kept other secrets with your own friends? Remember how your parents or teachers or older siblings told you not to care about the silly secrets other people shared? This is a primitive fear, one that starts young, and no amount of logic or sense can allay it.

Of course our fear of secrecy, especially the secrecy of the rich and powerful, isn't entirely of our own making. I'm certain that many of the ideas we have about various secret societies and occult movements have been planted in our minds by those same groups, to keep unwanted attention off them, or at least to obscure the common and practical truths about them in a fog of paranoia and conspiracy. To protect their secret place, some primitive tribes would position skulls or talismans around the perimeter to scare people away. In *The Name of the Rose*, Umberto Eco describes a secret library protected by a mirror that would frighten any medieval monk who saw it.

I mean, if you were a member of an elite group, earning an enormous amount of money and wielding power over entire countries, which route would you take to keep your position safe? Would you go public, publishing your bank balance in the media and going on Oprah to explain why the general public should not bother applying? Or would you simply – and easily – create an aura of danger by dropping a handful of vaguely sinister sound bites in obedient newspapers and websites?

In the end it's a watertight safety blanket: those who are not scared off simply become known as paranoid conspiracy theorists, their opinions and arguments discounted as the crazy ramblings of social misfits who never got enough fresh air as children!

So that's the first thing to understand when dealing with any kind of secret or occult society or practice: they are not intrinsically evil just because they keep their business private. They are not evil because they are rich or elitist. If this were the case, we'd be exorcising and consecrating every corporate boardroom from here to Wall Street. Privacy is frustrating and can sometimes hide abuses of power and perversions of morality – but not always.

The lure of hidden knowledge

The first thing to do when looking at hidden or occluded knowledge is to ask a simple question: why is it hidden?

Well, why is anything hidden? The answer takes us right back to the kindergarten playground. We hide things that we don't want other people to have. We hide things we want to keep all to ourselves. We hide things to satisfy those animal hoarding instincts we still have. In other words, we hide things because we're selfish.

This entire book is based on knowledge that has been hoarded, kept secret, by men whose motives for doing so were almost entirely selfish. And boy, have they played dirty! Here's their recipe. (Write it down if you're a megalomaniac – it'll come in useful one day when you're running your own banana republic in the Caribbean.)

Step one: declare certain rites and rituals open to men only. You've effectively removed half your competition in a single stroke. Next, decree that this knowledge is only attainable by those wealthy enough to engage in expensive formal study, and suddenly you've removed 90 percent of your remaining male opposition. Finally tag on a clause about needing to be Jewish or Catholic or circumcised or redheaded or Afrikaans or of royal Zulu blood, and you're left with about five people, with whom you can happily share the riches and prestige of your trade.

That's where the word 'cabal' comes from: Kabbalah was one of the most fiercely secret and protected of these beliefs, and so its very name became a synonym for elitism and exclusivity.

Of course the men dominating these elites often hinted that they were keeping their secrets for the benefit of humanity at large, as if this knowledge was a fearsome beast that they were taming and wrangling through great personal suffering and sacrifice. Please. Secrets are never kept to benefit humanity. When nuclear fission was discovered, we suddenly had the capacity to obliterate each other at the touch of a button. Governments with the technology did their utmost to keep it hidden. Thousands of warheads later, nukes are the world's worst-kept secret.

No, from pharmaceutical patents to religious dogma, secrets are kept for personal enrichment and power. But the greatest power lies not in products or money, but in knowledge. With the right knowledge, human beings can become godlike in this crude little world. It's a primitive pay-off, but it draws an enormous number of people towards it.

You bought this book because it offered a testimony to the survival of the soul. It is a book that preaches patience and acceptance of death, and the humility that comes with recognizing that we are like specks of dust moving up and down a wonderful sunbeam. But it is also a book that offers you a small amount of power: power over your fear of death, power over your confusion about the purpose of life.

However, this book is a source of power moderated and guided by control and humility, and when did people ever want control and humility? We want power because we have so little, and when we want it, we want it all. We want instant results, spectacular results.

If you're trying to lose weight, and have been going to gym and eating rabbit food covered in fat-free salad dressing for years, and have only lost a couple of kilos, don't you dream about a pill that will transform you? If you were offered that pill, and told about possible uncomfortable side-effects (and a very, very tiny chance of death), wouldn't you jump at it, rather than spending another year slogging away? Of course you would! You'd know the pill was full of dodgy chemicals, and that gym and salad would be much better for you, but would you care?

In other words, you'd throw caution to the winds. As if wielding a great spiritual and psychological credit card, you buy now and worry about payment later.

But payment always comes. Every day, somewhere in the world, Faust sells his soul to one devil or another. It might be the devil of addiction or greed, or it might be the ravenous devil of cruelty and emotional perversion, but the devil will have his due, and when he does, Faust is in deep, deep trouble.

Proceed with caution ...

If you were ever told by your parents that if you didn't eat your carrots you were going to get scurvy, then you have first-hand experience of the educational power of fear! You were left with a vague, horrible notion of your face falling off if you didn't wolf down those floppy, tasteless veggies.

It's a teaching technique we encounter far more than we realize. Not studying? Do you want to end up like poor Mr Smith over at the Salvation Army? You're going to that new club? Isn't that where that poor girl was chloroformed and sold to a passing Taiwanese fishing boat?

And somewhere, very early on, we pick up the same message about occluded knowledge, about 'the occult': if you read an esoteric book about it, even see a fragment of one of its rituals, your soul is lost and you are sliding down the steep path towards eternal damnation and hellfire! The prejudice saturates our Western culture, unspoken but almost universally accepted: exposure to any belief not sanctioned by Rome, Jerusalem or Mecca results in immediate and spectacular frenzies of chicken murder and virgin-tampering.

So does study of secret knowledge always lead to evil? Is it a path that, once trodden, inevitably leads to disaster? The short answer is no. But this entire field of knowledge has been abused and misrepresented and misunderstood because of too many short answers, so an explanation is in order.

Most people who become interested in secret or lost knowledge do so with good intentions. Perhaps they are trying to find a path to God that they don't feel is being offered by traditional religion. Perhaps they want to help the people around them.

Perhaps they want to learn how to heal, or cast protective spells around those they love. But what is it that's said about good intentions and the road to hell?

This is why we all have to watch ourselves carefully if we choose to start exploring the occluded world. We all have good intentions, but it is just too easy to get sucked into something without being fully aware of its potential pitfalls. This is true of so many aspects of our lives: one day we look up and wonder how on earth we got here, and recognize with sadness that it's nothing like we hoped or wanted.

Sometimes the risks are obvious. Climbing an ice face in the Himalayas is obviously a dangerous thing to do, and so climbers rope themselves together and climb in stages, well anchored to the ice. But when these dangers are less clear, less physical, we become reckless and assume we no longer need the spiritual or psychological versions of climbing harnesses.

It's a typically human reaction, and typically foolhardy. Because the truth about occult exploration is that if we're going to emerge undamaged, with our souls intact, we have to check in with ourselves the whole time. Earlier in this book I recommended that you should question your motives every so often, stop when you reach a fork in your path and give it a good thinking over. The same applies a hundredfold where hidden knowledge is concerned. Ask yourself: am I still walking in the light, or is it getting a little dim? Do I feel comfortable with this or not? Am I doing this to find myself and so find God, or am I doing this to make myself bigger and more important?

I'm no climber, but I gather that most of the deaths that happen on the upper slopes of Mount Everest occur for one of two reasons. First, people become confused and disoriented with altitude sickness, and make fatal mistakes. Second, their vanity or machismo drives them to take risks – for example, attempting a summit despite the threat of bad weather or the warnings of their Sherpas – and to insist that they know what they're doing.

These are dangers very relevant to the study of the occult. Both the arrogant student and the cautious one risk fatal consequences, reaching a point where their bodies and minds simply can't cope. In other words, it is vital to be humble enough to question ourselves regularly, and strong enough to remain spiritually and emotionally intact.

If you push out to sea in a boat, and you don't know how to navigate but are too arrogant to ask for directions, you're going one way.

... but proceed all the same

What's your comfort zone? It takes honesty to admit you have one, greater honesty to admit to yourself what it is. We all have them: we settle for second best, and rationalize our decision to back down from life's challenge. Life is hard, we tell ourselves with a stoic little sigh; what's important is to be a good and dutiful person rather than a fulfilled one; happy endings are just Hollywood lies ...

In other words, we lie to ourselves. And why would we do such a thing? Out of fear. Fear causes us to look down, to surrender, to conform, to believe half-truths. Racism is fear born out of ignorance and a refusal to expand our hearts and minds. We talk about the love of money, but it is not love, merely the fear of poverty and loneliness. We look up at God, and then back down, because we fear that embarking on the long path towards enlightenment will take more of us than we are willing to give.

Because we fear the answers to the huge questions that exist in the world, we wrap ourselves up tight in our safety blankets, our comfort zones. We conform and keep our heads down, stay under the radar, as life tries to get us to commit to what we believe. If God exists and our lives are judged, how could you possibly go on living the life you currently inhabit? Why aren't you selling all your possessions and giving all your money to the poor? Why do you carry on watching movies and having long lunches when you have so little time left to dedicate to God and your fellow human beings? The questions chime on and on like great bells, and we block our ears.

Sometimes we cling to a single path because it mercifully removes all that nasty and confusing choice. We fear the forks in the path, and follow those who seem to know where they're going. Although we are walking through a staggeringly beautiful land, we are terrified of stepping off the path.

Too often religion is a single path. It is well trodden and wide, and so seems safe and permanent, but what opportunity do you have of exploring a country when your road has no branches or detours? I admire people who follow their faith with openness and discipline built on reason and education, but there are as many, if not more, who fixate on their faith because they are afraid of themselves. They have locked themselves, their ego, into a cage of ritual and belief, because they are terrified that their desires, the secret whispers of their souls, will burst out and force them to change their entire world view. In other words, they are afraid of change and of growth.

I see it all the time. Jews are afraid to study the New Testament. Christians are afraid to study the Veda. Muslims are afraid of scepticism and debate about the details of the Koran. But in reality, what are they all afraid of? Perhaps of losing their way, or losing their sense of who they are. It takes courage, this exploration, but just as God gave us faith, He gave us brains and the ability to question.

So remember: *In exploring hidden knowledge, you are not automatically risking your eternal soul.* We are here to learn. It is our job to learn, and our duty. But most importantly, failing to learn, or cutting ourselves off from particular sources of knowledge because a religious or social elite has told us to, can leave us unprotected from the real dangers in the world. Or, indeed, create new ones. I've been accused of devil-worship in the past by fundamentalist Christians who wanted to silence what they considered evil. And once you embark on that path, you're squarely on the road that ends in Nazi-style book-burning and apartheid-style banning.

Perhaps a runny nose is the best way to illustrate this.

Most doctors will tell you that children need to get dirty. They need to play in mud and pick their noses and eat ants, and all the other apparently nasty things little children get up to. It is an essential part of growing up healthily, because it builds their immune systems. Children who grow up pampered and coddled in spotlessly clean air-conditioned apartments, where everything is glass and stainless steel, can often end up being sickly or allergic to apparently everything.

Likewise our world is dirty and noisy and messy. We need to get our knees scuffed and taste mud in order to learn and grow stronger. Perhaps I'm being too unforgiving on religions that bar their followers from learning more about hidden rites. Perhaps they want to protect their followers from hurt and harm in the way that parents in those glass-and-steel high-rise apartments want to protect their children. But the fact remains that they leave their faithful unequipped to face the harsh realities that life can throw at them. They are leaving them vulnerable to the darkness that occurs as naturally as dirt in our world.

Who's afraid of the big bad ego?

Pride comes before a fall. Lucifer and his rebel angels became vain, and paid the price. People who want to delve deeper into the hidden secrets of our world often do so for selfish reasons. It's not surprising then that the human ego has been branded by priests, scholars and philosophers as something destructive. Religion teaches us to crush it. Psychology tells us to keep it balanced. Our parents tell us to stop looking at ourselves in the mirror so darned much!

But the ego, like everything else about us, is God-given. Without egos there would be no artists, no great orators, no groundbreaking explorers or medical pioneers. It's what we *do* with our egos that matters, and this has nothing to do with God or Satan or religion or the occult. It's got everything to do with how we choose to live.

To blame ego for the world's ills, to use it as a scapegoat for our failings, denies the power of our minds. Between your ears you have the most extraordinary computer and counsellor in the known universe. To suggest that the ego is stronger or more cunning than that amazing machine is to condone moral weakness. It is to say, 'The devil made me do it!' instead of 'I forgot God, and so I did it.'

Belinda Silbert is a witch!

In 2004 I hit the headlines in Cape Town after a show of mine was disrupted by a group of American evangelical hecklers. It was standard stuff – Belinda Silbert is a witch, she worships spirits, she summons the dead, she uses leaded petrol and eats at McDonald's, blah blah blah – but nonetheless it was upsetting because it exposed me, up close and personal, to the kind of self-righteous ignorance and prejudice that often resorts to violence to get its way.

But are they entirely wrong? Is there something in what I do that could be construed as 'evil' or dangerous or Satanic or heretical? In other words, where do you draw the line between acceptable occult practice and the nasty stuff?

Perhaps it's best to distinguish between occultism and mysticism. They overlap a great deal – after all, much of mystical lore is hidden or occult – but there is a profound difference in intention. Very simply (and perhaps this is a generalization), the exploration of hidden or occult knowledge is often so as to overturn the secrets of the universe for personal power and gain, and most importantly to gain power over other people. Mysticism is the search for those secrets fuelled by a desire to be one with God, or to help others.

By this basic definition, I am a mystic. I have studied occult lore and have walked dark and hidden paths, but my intention was never to lurk there for the benefit of my vanity and self-esteem.

And as for the charge that I worship spirits, well, let me ask you this. Would you worship your neighbours just because you can hear them crashing about upstairs and you sometimes pick up their telephone calls on your line? I rest my case! I worship God, because God alone is worthy of worship.

Everyone's got one nowadays

In 2002 academics David Barrett and Todd Johnson published *A Statistical Approach to the World's Religious Adherents*. Their goal was simple but enormously ambitious: a census of who was worshipping what and where. Their process was complicated and at times fairly rigid, and while some of their data was open to debate, one striking trend emerged: a mass movement towards new religions.

The pair defined these new religions as 'twentieth-century new religions, new religious movements, radical new crisis religions, and non-Christian syncretistic mass religions, all founded since 1800 and most since 1945, mostly Asian in origin and membership but increasingly with worldwide followings'. A broad sweep, to be sure. But, you might wonder, surely the New Religion pool can't be that deep once you've removed all the Christians (Catholic, Protestant, Independent), Muslims, Baha'i, Hindus, Sikhs, Jains, Buddhists, Zoroastrians, Jews, Confucians, Taoists, Shintoists and Spiritists from the equation?

Well, try some of these numbers on for size!

According to Barrett and Johnson, there are 28,400 followers of New Religions in Africa, 158,000 in Europe, 622,000 in Latin America, 66,500 in Australia and Oceania, and a whopping 845,000 in North America. But dwarfing them all is Asia, with over 100 million New Religion believers! Critics suggest that this figure is greatly exaggerated by a very loose definition of New Religion in Asia's complex and fluid religious world, but even if we halve that figure, you're still left with the population of South Africa!

In other words, it's safe to say that there are 1,7 million people (outside Asia!) who follow a faith invented in the last hundred years. Some of these faiths are based on ancient lore, others are downright stupid: the United Kingdom now recognises Jedi (the hocus-pocus pseudo-mysticism of the Star Wars movies) as a genuine religion, which suggests that this is all degenerating into a real dog show.

But why the sudden explosion of religions? Why are there over 2000 different religions practised in the UK alone?

I believe the reason lies partly in the convenience these religions offer their followers. Faith and spiritual development take hard work and humility, and in today's world – especially the materialistic, vain West – many people are frightened off by those requirements. They want quick solutions to problems humanity has wrestled with for tens of thousands of years. They can't bring themselves to face just how tiny we are, how insignificant in comparison to the huge processes of the Hereafter. They want a religion in which they – and not God – are the star, in which their self-esteem is boosted, in which time-consuming meditation is cut down to a minimum. In short, they want potted religion.

Of course, this is a recipe for superficiality and commercialization. Any faith that you can switch on and off, depending on how busy your day is or whether you're feeling a little down and need cheering up, is simply a crutch, and has nothing to do with God or belief. In the Middle Ages Catholics were Catholic all day every day. They thought about God and sin constantly. Each mundane event in their day was a test of their faith, or a confirmation of God's presence on earth. You don't nail yourself to a cross once a year (as one South American sect did) if you don't believe in what you're doing! But today even some Catholics are becoming faithful-by-convenience: a weekly confession absolves them, and off they go, unrepentant and unthinking, to continue doing the same things to which they've just confessed. The moment convenience starts making demands on our faith, the spirituality is bleached out of it.

Laziness is certainly one factor, but ignorance is another. I see it all the time, especially on the fringes of the New Age beliefs, where people become lost and confused, and become fixated on a single guru or mentor. Suddenly, instead of focusing on their souls and on God, they become preoccupied with all the paraphernalia that they think they need!

It makes me crazy the way people approach this process back-to-front. You've now got people going to the library and taking out books on Wicca and teaching themselves to be high priests or priestesses, when they know absolutely nothing about themselves as human or spiritual beings. You have to be pretty clueless to think you can perform open-heart surgery when you've never treated a paper cut on your own finger. But you also have to be arrogant, and unfortunately many modern religions encourage this self-centred attitude. Even charismatic Christianity has gone this way: once we were not fit to wash the feet of Jesus Christ, but today we're encouraged to be His best pal, as if we were His equal.

Occult religions – Wicca and the Neo-Pagans

Spirituality has become an accessory. But it has also become a crutch, and too often people in the West (who might have lost their sense of direction or might be feeling hollow because they are young, alone, perhaps the victims of a messy divorce) latch on to a potted religion in the hope that it will make them important, suddenly give them some of the insight and power they so badly want and need. And of course the result is commercialization, and widespread misunderstanding of practices and intentions.

In talking about Wicca and new Pagan beliefs, I must stress again that I have a major problem with people hijacking the practices of other cultures. Apart from being morally sloppy and revealing intellectual and emotional neediness, it verges on heresy. But mostly it's often just hypocritical and tacky: white Americans waged genocidal war on the native inhabitants of their continents, but now that many Native Americans are degraded to alcoholic nomads, the descendants of these settlers adopt Native American belief systems with scant recognition of the collective horror that still hangs over that world.

I also take serious exception to people dashing off to sweat-lodges or teepees where they smoke enormous amounts of dope and fall about getting in touch with the Earth Mother or Great Spirit or whatever pseudo-spiritual emotional crutch they're searching for. Like wow, man, what's with these magic mushrooms!

But apart from the fact that these spiritual tourists are making fools of themselves, they're also adopting another culture for entirely the wrong reasons. Spiritual or mystical practices are intricately bound to culture. They're not products for sale, for the wandering misfit to try on for size or experiment with. Most culture's religious or spiritual traditions have existed for thousands of years, and that energy, created by generations repeating their own sacred forms and experiencing God in their own way, is unique from culture to culture.

The current fad in the West is to experiment with the beliefs of primal cultures, such as the ancient customs of Africa or the East. The result? An astonishing number of fakes wondering about with dirty hair and smelly breath! South Africa has its own fair share: white sangomas who have grown tired of being plumbers and chartered accountants and now seek fulfilment in adopting a culture to which they have no right, and that their immediate ancestors did their best to wipe out.

Whenever I am approached by these lost souls I urge them to go back to their own tradition, to find what is good in it without being sucked into the dogma. So often we forget that our own culture's faith (whatever that culture may be) was based on meditation and contemplation, but we reject what it has become. For instance, I know Catholics who have turned away from their faith because the power of its rituals has become lost or obscured through repetition. I encourage these people to return to the church and light candles between services, to perform their own sacred rituals in order to experience God – or at least God's peace and meditation – with none of the clutter and ego of human intervention.

That holiness is there, it's all around us, and you don't need to smoke a pipe of dodgy weeds in a yurt in Mongolia or sit naked in a Navajo sweat lodge to tap into the holiness. Go to church, to temple, to mosque. Go to a place resonating with holiness, be it a cathedral or mountainside, and listen.

Wicca was invented by a rather shady character called Gerald Gardner, who didn't help his religion's reputation by fraudulently claiming various academic qualifications. Like many instantly created belief systems, it borrows from many traditions – most of its style and aesthetics are lifted from ancient Celtic paganism – but on the whole it is a polyglot of magic, environmentalism and feminism.

The Celtic pagans – who saw God and nature as the same thing – were on the whole a very gentle people. It was central to their creed not to harm others or destroy the world around them; and modern pagans like the Wiccans embrace a similar philosophy, and are often gentle and intelligent people. However, considering that the Romans and Vikings were also pagans, it's clear that paganism doesn't automatically rule out violent colonization and wholesale massacre!

In fact Wicca does seem open to a very wide range of interpretations. I even know someone who claims to be a Judeo-Wiccan, who worships the god of the Jewish Torah but performs all manner of pagan ceremonies.

Because Wicca is taking off in the suburbs of Europe and the United States, its rituals and dramatic costumes are coming to the attention of more traditional Christian citizens, who, either through fear or conviction, often accuse Wiccans of being Satanists. You know, all those black robes and pasty white faces …

But their fear is misplaced and misinformed. Wiccans are gentle people, often intelligent middle-class professionals who are searching for a more satisfying spiritual experience. Indeed, it seems fairly shortsighted for a follower of a faith that produced the Crusades or Islamo-fascism to criticize people who get together to greet the full moon or chant small spells for the benefit of others! Wicca is essentially benevolent, and it's easy to see why: the so-called 'three-fold law' holds that everything they do will be revisited on them three times over. If they practise good, they're in line for spiritual and emotional perks. If they act malevolently, they're in for a triple-whammy.

But in the end these people are not Celts. Under their robes they are wearing suits and wrist watches. And despite their best intentions, the practitioners of Wicca (itself a diluted religion) are diluting Celtic traditions even further. Their spells are losing power, and the original knowledge is fading, like a photocopy of a photocopy.

It's a kind of magic

No pagan religion would be particularly satisfying without a glamorous smattering of magic, or magick as the Wiccans insist on spelling it, which many groups practise in a fairly basic form.

Traditionally there were two branches of magic – high and low. High magic was performed by the wealthy, who had the time it took to indulge in long and elaborate ceremonies. In fact high magic dates back to the time of Solomon, when enormous, lavish rituals were performed, often just for the sake of intrigue and drama. High magic still survives today in the secret societies where lodges, secret handshakes and midnight rituals at exclusive resorts are the order of the day. This is Harry Potter in a tuxedo …

But not everyone can afford to go to the local version of Hogwarts, and this is how low magic started in the early Middle Ages. It was the craft of herbalists and mystics (or witches, depending on which side of the gallows you're standing). As you can imagine, these were simple people without the time or money to indulge in the intricate ceremonies of high magic, and as a result they created quick fixes, or what we today know as spells. Where the aristocracy or priest class might perform fertility rituals or try to predict blood lines, lowly witches and herbalists catered for more simple desires: love, wealth and happiness!

Kabbalah

The chapter after this deals exclusively with the ancient mystical philosophy of Judaism that we call Kabbalah, and so I offer no explanation or examination of it here. But it serves as an excellent example of a mystical belief system that has been seized upon in the last few years by those looking for something new.

It seems that these days you can't read a single gossip column without discovering that some new teenage singing sensation has decided that she's going to become more spiritual, and has started 'practising Kabbalah'. Blurry paparazzi pictures show her looking demure and sombre in some frumpy clothes, and we're told that she's changed her life entirely (of course it might just be laundry day and she might have indigestion, but who's to say?)

Now I don't want to be mean about celebrities. I'm sure some of them are nice people. But just as is the case with politicians, you can't be a professional celebrity without a maniacal focus on money and fame. And it is often the case that people whose only religion is greed and self-promotion, and whose only gods are money and fame, come to a point in their lives when they recognize the terrible hollowness of their beliefs. They feel cut off, isolated and desperately shallow. They long for some link to an ancient and important tradition. They want to believe in something greater than themselves.

But not that much greater. We're still talking about people for whom the centre of the known universe is themselves!

In fact, to someone too vain to take the time to study it properly, Kabbalah seems like the perfect celebrity belief. There are very few Buddhist celebrities, and almost no overtly Christian or Muslim ones, perhaps because these religions preach humility, and urge their practitioners to surrender or be subservient to higher powers, be it the circle of life or God or Allah. But Kabbalah, seen simplistically, seems to offer privileged knowledge, promises access to a secret society open only to people who are spiritually or intellectually enlightened.

If Jedi can rate as a religion, then you might assume that Kabbalah can too. Certainly many of its new students (and I used the word in its loosest and most charitable sense) talk about it as if it were a religion; a few have been quoted as saying that they are 'converting to Kabbalah'. But Kabbalah is not a religion. It is a path of learning and enlightenment, a way of contemplating and wrestling with the complex mystical philosophies of Judaism. Yes, it contains the building blocks of religion, but it is no more a religion than is a PhD in molecular biology. The problem is that it is being taught by rabbis, and so people are mistaking it for a finished 'product', a complete religion.

Women and the occult

It's not a generalization to say that women form the vast majority of those who practise occult traditions, or who have embraced modern varieties like Wicca. From the witches of the Middle Ages to those free-spirited women one finds selling crystals and herbs in bohemian shops, women seem to dominate the para-religious world. Why should this be?

Firstly, women are disempowered. Since men wrested control of human society thousands of years ago, they have kept women in a subservient position as a way of holding on to power. People who have had their emotional and intellectual integrity denied, who are considered second-class citizens, will often turn to spiritual or religious beliefs: look, for example, at how often slave communities around the world clung to their spiritual practices or embraced new ones with such passion.

But often the traditional or formal religious practices are the domain of those same men who have forced women into a lower social status. And why would you, as a woman, aspire to the beliefs of the priest or bishop or druid who had condemned you and your sex to a life of servitude? Hence many women have traditionally followed their own path, studying rituals or herbs, or cobbling together pieces of formal religion to form their own belief system. It is no coincidence that the rise of feminism in the late 20th century mirrored a raised profile of Wicca and other occult practices: women were coming out of the closet spiritually.

Secondly, women are strong enough to deal with the forces they are exposed to, whereas men sometimes prove to be weak. Where a man will follow a path out of vanity or need, a woman will stop before she gets into trouble, because she has greater knowledge of her self and her motives. Where a man is more likely to want power for himself, a woman will want empowerment for those she loves.

People often try to analyse me, and end up projecting their beliefs or insecurities onto me. Astrologers tell me I'm tough and independent and creative because I'm an Aquarian. Numerologists tell me it's because my numbers stack up. New Agers ascribe it to crystals I supposedly have lying about in my house. But why am I tough and independent? I'll tell you: it's because I'm 5ft 2 and a woman!

Thirdly, women are drawn to the occult and mystical practices because they possess powers that men often don't. Women can access the higher vibrations – those of the spirit world, and similar planes – far more easily than men can. Women are often more capable of suspending their disbelief than men. Think of children playing by a river: how often isn't it the little girls who see fairies, and the little boys who throw pebbles at them for being 'girly'?

Hitler, Nazism and the New Age

Today's occult practices cover a range of moralities, from harmless (and perhaps naïve) pottering about with herbs and incantations to ritualized atrocities committed by deeply evil people and their sick acolytes. But those who do indulge in the hidden arts are a small minority. Some would argue they are a powerful minority (in the case of the Illuminati or the Freemasons), but the reality of everyday life is that you and I aren't affected by their rituals and beliefs: we don't have to give secret handshakes to our hairdresser just to get served, or spend a few hours chanting Latin at the Post Office when we've come to collect a package.

However, it is very important for all thinking people to understand the potential evil of certain occult practices, because the human animal is weak. Our minds are extraordinarily advanced in many ways, but in other ways we are terribly crude. Drink Coke! We see the white lettering on red, and forget all about Pepsi. Only R250,000 for a car? We accept the 'only' part, never thinking that to pay a quarter of a million rand for a car is obscene; that it could feed a hundred people for a year. Colin Powell and Tony Blair show the United Nations an artist's impression of Iraqi bio-terror factories, and the United States electorate and many in Europe go to war.

And we only need to look back two generations for the ultimate example of occult mutation on an international scale. The Second World War was a political struggle, the crushing of Fascism, but we can't help feeling it was a battle between good and evil, no less.

Many wars are fought in which victory for either side changes not much more than the politics in the region: think about the endless wars between England and France before the 20th century, or the countless little wars and coups in South America, where, as Colombian writer Gabriel Garcia Marquez said, only the colour of the uniforms changed. But the future of humanity, and the fate of our souls, hung on the outcome of World War Two.

Had Hitler won, Judaism and the Slavic peoples of Russia

would be extinct, burnt in the incinerators of Europe; Africa and south-east Asia would be enormous slave colonies, people worked to death or murdered for sport in the knowledge that there were plenty more. Many commentators have pointed out that victory for Hitler would have ushered in a new Dark Age, but this is an understatement: the barbarism of the Dark Ages didn't have massive transportation networks, poison gas, aircraft and control of vast resources.

And most importantly, the warlords of the Dark Ages were motivated by a lust for power and wealth, whereas Hitler was motivated by darker forces, and it is these forces we must recognize and understand, so that a similar abomination cannot rise again while we have the knowledge and power to stop it.

I know what you're thinking. You're rolling your eyes and getting ready to turn the page. Hitler and occult hoopla? Please, give me a break! That's on a par with those books that say Ronald Reagan was a lizard and that the moon-landing was faked, right?

But haven't you ever wondered how millions of educated, enlightened Germans could blindly follow a crazy little warlord, could ignore the all-too-obvious signs of mass killings, could believe they would beat the combined forces of the United States and Russia? And why, if Nazism was all about Germany and nationalism, was the German flag overshadowed by the hooked cross, the Swastika, itself an ancient mystic or occult symbol, and why were millions of patriotic German citizens shipped to the gas chambers just because they were Jews? Where did Hitler's obsession with racial purity come from, his desire to build a super-race of blond, blue-eyed Aryan warriors?

The answers lie in the occult, and recent research is revealing a fascinating but chilling picture of Hitler as a man obsessed and infatuated with ancient traditions and rituals, many stemming from the same sources that feed some of today's New Age practices.

It seems that Hitler rejected traditional Christianity in his teens, and while still a young man discovered like-minded people who introduced him to the occult. Any lasting notions of traditional religion would certainly have been destroyed by the horror of trench warfare in World War One, where many men far more balanced than Hitler were filled with contempt for the weak, passive God of the Bible who allowed men to be slaughtered like this.

But Hitler's contempt for Christianity also seems to stem from a belief that it had weakened humanity. In his book *The Nazis and the Occult*, D. Sklar quotes Hitler denouncing Christianity on the grounds that it 'only added the seeds of decadence such as forgiveness, self-abnegation, weakness, false humility and the very denial of the evolutionary laws of survival of the fittest'.

The essence of the beliefs that Hitler surrounded himself with in the 1920s was a certainty that humanity was about to evolve into a new species, a higher and more noble species, powered by its will rather than 'outdated' ideas of morality. This nobility and elevated status therefore had nothing to do with Biblical concepts of right and wrong; Hitler's new human being, the product of the New Age, would reject what he called 'dirty and degrading' notions like conscience and morality. Conscience, he said, was a Jewish invention.

The new humanity would also not have 'the burden of free will'; in other words, it would no longer have to think for itself, and the first signs of this were clearly visible in Nazi Germany as a group consciousness began to emerge. Think of the massive Nuremberg rallies where even cynical independent people found themselves under a spell, saluting and chanting in unison with tens of thousands of followers.

One would think that this sort of mass-consciousness has little to do with the will that Hitler spoke of so often, but will to

Nazism was a collective will, the driving force behind a people (*volk*) intent on shaping their own destiny, an idea drawn straight out of occult texts. The hatred of Jews, which we often think was the impetus for Hitler's experiment, was only the natural product of this collective idea. Jews have always asserted their separateness, both as independent people and as a religious or racial group. 'God's chosen people' have never wanted nor tried to integrate fully with the populations where they have found themselves around the world. And this independence, this assertion of individuality, came into direct conflict with Hitler's theories of collective obedience.

Of course this sort of national indoctrination can't happen without the population being open to it. And the Germans of the 1930s, perhaps without knowing it, were ripe for an occult conversion. Most of them would have grown up surrounded by fairytales and myths stemming from ancient Nordic or Germanic traditions, full of magic and heroism, rings and swords and national destiny. One of the most successful propaganda images of Hitler was of him in armour on a horse, tapping straight into medieval ideas of knights on quests. It's no coincidence that one of the occult paths Hitler took was obsessive research into the Holy Grail, what we know as the cup of Christ at the last supper, but which the Nazis believed was a symbol of racial purity (Jesus was not considered a Jew, but a Gnostic of pure blood), or as the 'philosopher's stone', a source of god-like self-knowledge given to humanity by Lucifer when he fell from heaven.

I believe that Hitler used his occult learning to tap into frequencies that could overwhelm the senses and mind, as he did at the great rallies. Certainly the obsession of various groups in the Reich seems to have been fuelled by a dark energy, presumably springing from rituals and beliefs: the ruthless persecution of its enemies by the Gestapo took more than a good work ethic and diligence; and those who fought against SS groups in Europe report their almost berserk bravery, fighting with skill and suicidal determination, often to the last man.

In the end it was fitting, in occult terms, that Hitler committed suicide. The Russians who found his bunker considered it an act of cowardice, but to Hitler it would have been part of an ancient pagan ritual. Indeed, his suicide took place on the eve of Walpurgisnacht, 30 April, the pagan ancestor of the modern Halloween and a festival still celebrated by modern Wiccans. But there was more to it than the date: that Hitler died with his wife Eva Braun indicated a ritualistic death, following an ancient doctrine allegedly taught by the original protectors of the Grail, who demanded suicide in pairs. Also found in the bunker were Josef Goebbels and his wife.

Why worry?

But why should we in the 21st century concern ourselves with a historical freak occurrence like the Nazi era? Surely if someone like Hitler arrived today we'd see through him? And in any case, we aren't as saturated with Germanic myth as were his German followers, so his spell wouldn't work on us, would it?

No, it probably wouldn't, and it is very unlikely that the neo-Nazi movements around the world, even those currently engaged in occult research, will threaten us in the future. But our world is as open as ever to attacks on our independence and individuality. Some New Age beliefs today urge us to abandon our individuality to a greater good. Those who want to hold on to their traditional beliefs are criticized by the New Agers, and called arrogant and selfish. And suddenly we are on a slippery slope towards Nazi-style interrogations about loyalty and racial purity.

I'm certainly not saying that New Age practitioners are Hitler incarnate, not at all. But there are those in the movement who have a slightly shaky track record of not condemning his genocide, or of making anti-Semitic statements. And despite what benign and benevolent New Age groups might say and do, at the core of their beliefs is that familiar view of the evolution of humanity being in terms of power and action, rather than the evolution of the soul towards God. I would urge New Age believers to reaffirm their commitment to God and to the whole of humanity, and to be rigorous about questioning their own motives.

So where does this leave us? Let's see:

We all watch the same films, and so have the same ideas about heroism (it's okay to kill other people if they look different or threaten you), family (Dad's a useless lump, Mom's neurotic, families are a bad idea all round), and romance (love is all you need, it's worth dying for, it's more important than intelligence and ambition and reason).

We all respond to advertising, even if we like to think we don't.

We all listen to the same music.

We are encouraged to have an opinion on politics, usually the same opinion as those we aspire to be.

We are encouraged to reject conscience and morality, and to 'follow our hearts' – from Bridget Jones to the office romance to Woolworths advertisements urging 'be more you' – in other words, indulge ourselves.

Increasingly we are all speaking the same language.

Increasingly we are worshipping the same god: money.

In other words, we're ripe for the taking. So far the dictators have been businessmen (Bill Gates, whom we obey without thinking; Rupert Murdoch, whose media puppet-show we never consider questioning; those nameless billionaires whose impact on our lives we can't even imagine, but who have a say in every aspect of our existence), but the military aspect will come. And when it does, will we be ready to assert out humanity?

Consider for a moment that the word 'unanimous' – the type of absolute consensus we all think is such a good idea in politics and our daily relationships – literally means 'one-souled'. Eventually we will be one-souled, when we reach God, but this state of being – or more accurately, the end of individual being – has nothing to do with enlightenment and living good lives on earth or arranging crystals so as to keep wrinkles away or your toilet smelling fresh or whatever the hell they are supposed to do. When we become 'unanimous' with God, all of this, everything in this book, will seem so simplistic as to be irrelevant.

> Any belief system that demands conformity (even in
> the name of a better future) will eventually demand
> that we reject those people who refuse to conform.
> And the most effective way to reject something is to
> remove it from view: in short, extermination.

Satanism

And now, finally, the bit you've been waiting for all along!

I might be critical of certain aspects of Wicca and the New Age movement, but I am not opposed to any of them. However no moral human being can tolerate Satanism.

Satanism is about one thing and one thing only: personal power. But this doesn't mean its ranks are filled with megalomaniacs or control freaks. On the contrary, Satanism is awash with sad, ineffectual little people: the powerless, the weak, the small, the insignificant. Like moths to a flame they are drawn to it, spurred on by the prospect of having power over the people they feel so rejected by.

Of course it's not only emotional need and spiritual numbness that pull people towards Satanism. In my experience drugs play a large role. Now I know I'm sounding like those Mother Grundies who blame everything on the Demon Liquor that the Young People drink at Night Clubs, but my moral condemnation of the use and abuse of chemicals is based on the purely physical change they bring about in people. More specifically, drugs and alcohol lower your vibrational level to a point where a Satanic or Luciferian consciousness can quite easily take hold of you. Again, this sounds like something a fire-and-brimstone preacher would bellow from the pulpit, but let me explain it in terms that sound slightly less apocalyptic.

Basically, if you've ever been drunk or under the influence of something like marijuana, you'll recognize the feeling of everything being slow and dense and muted. Consequences suddenly become irrelevant, you feel detached from your actions, and more specifically you become detached from your personality. The desire for physical sensations – specifically sexual and violent ones – is increased, and at the same time rational thought becomes not only difficult, but also deeply irritating! And this is the vibration, the frequency, of the dark consciousness and of the Grey Zones.

Wiccans are not Satanists. Goths – those miserable young people who slouch around dressed in black, feeling persecuted and superior – are not Satanists. Yes, they need to scrub the black makeup off, get a haircut and get a job, but that's all!

No, Satanists are a breed apart. They have fallen through the basement of the darkest occult rites. Their souls have been numbed to their own pain and the pain of the people they are abusing. They are anaesthetized, soul-sick. And this numbness demands that they need more: as with drugs and pornography, the addict needs a bigger and better fix, and more extreme experiences to conjure the same sensation; and so the depraved acts begin, and the descent into animal obscenities has begun ...

Are traditional religions responsible for Satanism?

This is a very touchy subject, and one best left up to psychologists and sociologists. But it can't be a coincidence that Satanism is usually most prevalent in conservative communities, where strong Christian values are imposed on young people.

I often feel that both charismatic Christianity and orthodox Judaism focus on Satan to such a degree that they end up drawing undue attention to him; and whatever you draw that much attention to, you're going to manifest. In fact, I've been to some services where the devil was given so many of his dues that I was left wondering who exactly was being worshipped, and where God was in the equation! God is great, says the sermon, but that Satan – well! He's everywhere. He can turn husband against wife, brother against brother; he can disguise himself in beauty; he can corrupt even the purest heart and tempt even the most resolute soul. Suddenly Satan is the star of the show, the bad guy getting all the great scenes and all the memorable lines.

Know your enemy

But who is this devil who so much of the world has fought and agonized over for thousands of years? Why, despite millennia of warnings and stern lectures about staying away from reddish blokes with cloven hoofs, are we still vague about whether or not he exists, and if he does, who he is? Old Nick, Lucifer, Beelzebub, Mephistopheles, The Prince of Darkness (that other one, that is, not Ozzy Osbourne …): are they one and the same?

We have to be very clear about two things. Firstly: *Satan exists.* Just because the astral manifests as grey and dank, and not a pit of hellish fire ruled over by a goat-like fellow with a pointy beard and wickedly twirled moustache, it doesn't follow that the traditional notion of Satan is entirely wrong. Satan exists, and Satan exists in our world. I will discuss this further shortly.

Secondly: *Lucifer is not Satan.* The history and theology of

Satan is enormously complicated, and this is not the time or place to plunge into that particular bog. Suffice it to say that the word 'Satan' has various origins. The Egyptians had a god named Set, who mirrored in many ways the later ideas that developed about the source of the universe's evil. Perhaps closer to biblical sources and times, we come across the Hebrew word 'Ha-Satan', and many non-Jews make the mistake of assuming a direct link between the Bible's Satan and this being, which, literally translated, refers to an 'accuser'. But in the ancient Hebraic tradition, Ha-Satan is the leader of a group of prosecuting angels who confront all souls after death, something like a more ferocious version of the Council. Rather look to the being named Sama-el for the Hebrew Satan. Even its name, Sama-el, is filled with potency, and to be frank it's not a word I like to use very much if I can help it.

But naturally the myths and beliefs – and even the physical names and words – of various middle-eastern religions have blurred and cross-pollinated, and it's possible that that distinctions have been lost. Where theological debate and translation is concerned, anything can happen! Is the Christian Satan a misunderstood Ha-Satan? Was Lucifer, the fallen angel, a chief prosecutor at some stage? Remember, wherever you find human language, you find misunderstanding. For example, since childhood you've known the phrase 'hocus pocus'. You know it refers to magic (either real or show-ground fakery), and you know it started out as a magical incantation. But what are its origins? The prevailing theory reveals the slippery nature of words: some linguists believe that the phrase dates back the Middle Ages, when peasants would crowd into churches and cathedrals, standing on tip-toes at the back and craning to hear the words of the priest. Services were in Latin, and during communion the priest would hold up the bread and declare 'Hoc est corpus meum!' – this is my body. It's very likely that those at the back of the church (who understood no Latin) would mishear, or try to repeat the phrase later and manage only a rough estimation. Hoc est corpus meum? Hocus pocus! And since the blessing of the church was regarded as an almost magical charm, any 'holy phrase' like this would have been taken back to farms and villages and clung on to as a way of warding off demons and crop failures.

But then again, there are some similarities between the Hebrew dark lord and the angel we know as Lucifer. In Hebrew one of the names of God is 'El', and any words that describe a creature or possession of God ends in 'el', as in the case of 'Israel' or God's great angels Michael and Gabriel. By this logic, Samael is still a creature of God, a favoured being as Lucifer was before his plunge.

The story of the fallen angels is almost universal, but to this day many of its darker implications are ignored or under-researched. Babylonian myth, the Koran, even the standard Christian Bible describe how the fallen angels came to earth and interbred with human women to create a race of giants, known as either the Nephilim or Rephaim, which was eventually wiped out in the great flood. Giants? The offspring of angels? I don't blame you if this is news to you: those passages in the Bible (Isaiah 26 and Genesis 6 are good examples) are as clear as day, and yet they are brushed aside by traditional religious doctrine. And what questions they raise! Were those heavenly children the gods of the Egyptians? Did they build the pyramids of Egypt and Central America? Does their line still exist today? Will science ever find their DNA?

So the fourteen rebel angels, who had tried to ensoul their own race of creations, in other words had tried to be God, were offered a deal. God, the ultimate Godfather, offered them a deal they couldn't refuse! Either they could go to earth to be reincarnated here, with a double karmic penalty, or it was a long walk off a short pier, with the heavenly equivalent of concrete slippers. Human life, or sleep with the fishes ...

Thirteen of the angels chose reincarnation, but Lucifer, the Light Bearer, the Morning Star, refused to cop a plea. Why should God be the only consciousness? Why should He be the only creator?

And so God sent Lucifer to earth, as an unwilling instrument of God's plan for us.

A favourite challenge levelled at religion by both atheists and theological agitators is this: if God is all-powerful, why doesn't He just destroy Lucifer? If He's so good, why does He let evil exist?

But this is book-burning logic. In the end, God sent Lucifer to rule over our world so that we could actively choose between good and evil. In an evil world, choosing good is always the more difficult, and therefore more worthy, choice. The final joke was on Lucifer, because he has no real power. He is a ruler – in hell, on earth, wherever you believe he exists – but one who is utterly unable to stop his alleged subjects from turning against him as soon as they recognize God or start to search for their souls. It is literally impossible for Satan to claim souls for eternity. Because eternity is God. He's borrowed those souls from God for a quick game of toy soldiers.

But this doesn't deny that evil and the Luciferian consciousness have very destructive powers in the real, everyday world. They might not have the power to stop the soul's progression towards God, but they are masters at causing pain and suffering in this world, be it through war or addiction or domestic violence or vanity. I believe that evil is rising in our world, because it feeds on anger and violence.

But, I hear you say, surely our world can't be more violent or full of suffering than it was a hundred or a thousand years ago? Perhaps not, but television and our ability to know about anger and violence from all over the world are new. A thousand years ago French knights might have been enraged by the presence of Muslims in Jerusalem, or Muslim scholars might have been appalled at the homicidal chutzpah of the Crusaders coming at them out of Europe. As for the rest, people's gripes were about local earls, crops, nosy neighbours and that pesky pig that kept breaking down the fence and raising hell in the vegetable patch.

But today our negativity feeds on a buffet of fears and resentments: someone living on a smallholding in New Zealand (whose only concerns should be his crops, family, neighbours and local government) can stay awake at night worrying about American imperialism, Islamic extremism, Chinese military ambitions, the Russian AIDS pandemic, African instability, North Korean and Iranian nuclear capabilities, global warming, water shortages in Africa, polio outbreaks in Eastern Europe.

The list goes on and on, and for every item on it, our depressed Kiwi will wonder: What does it all mean? And of course there is no certain answer to any of this, which leads to doubt and a feeling of powerlessness. In short, it leads to fear and pessimism. History and the laws of probability tell us that our Kiwi is far more likely to die of old age or be trampled by sheep or drown in his dipping pen than he is to be hit by an Iranian nuclear missile, and yet those impractical, unlikely phantoms dominate his thoughts and cause him to retreat further into himself, further away from God and the light of the world.

Another rebellion?
Playing devil's advocate for a moment might make me guilty of a ghastly pun at this stage in the book, but I've always been intrigued by the idea that the angels who fell had the freedom of choice to defy God. My research and beliefs tell me that only archangels have what we would consider free will, and so the

fourteen fallen angels must have been archangels, a fact born out by the Bible's naming of Lucifer as one of that elite group.

But here's the question: if archangels rebelled once, what's to say they won't do it again? Michael, Gabriel, the hard-core loyal lieutenants of God: to Christians and theologians of all faiths their loyalty is beyond question. But so was Lucifer's, once upon a time …

Obviously this is what television courtroom dramas call speculation. It's theological what-if, and has no purpose or use in our lives or world. But still, one can't help wondering what it would take for Michael and Gabriel (both good Sicilian names) to try to start their own *cosa nostra*, to defy the Godfather again. And who knows how much ammunition they'd have at their disposal? They might point at our militarized oppressive world and say, Don God, we gotta tell you, them creatures down there ain't looking too wonderful any more. And that's just earth: there is life all over our universe, and in all the universes created by God: it is a certainty that there are other planets or worlds far more awful than ours, which have gone far more awry.

More things in heaven and earth …
Remember, there is always more to learn. There are always other paths, other layers. Be modest enough to admit to ignorance, and be focused and mature enough to accept that only through learning can we lay any kind of claim to truth, however tiny a claim. Be cautious and adventurous in your explorations. But above all, remember to honour yourself, to ask your own opinion, and to give yourself the respect you deserve by being honest to yourself. If you manage these things, the world's hidden knowledge lies before you like a pearl waiting to be found. Don't be afraid of the oyster than hides the pearl: it is dark and slimy, and won't open without a struggle; but the final prize – if dealt with responsibly – is priceless.

9

Kabbalah for beginners

I've spent a good deal of time in this book explaining why it is important to think about what we believe, and to strive to appreciate the deeply satisfying logic in God's universe. I know that belief and logic seldom seem to have anything to do with each other, but you are lucky indeed when you can explain why you believe what you believe, in a way that is both logically sound and emotionally healthy.

So I think it's only fair that I begin this chapter – in which I explain my own belief system – with a logical explanation of why other religions and beliefs don't suit me. I owe you that much! Hopefully, if you haven't ever questioned your beliefs, it will help you to engage in that important process. Remember, questioning your faith doesn't imply doubt. We test things to make them stronger. (Just ask any crash-test dummy.) If our beliefs stand up to our questions and trials, then we embrace them even more fully.

The first of the great belief systems I would like to discuss is Buddhism. The day-to-day rites and disciplines of Buddhism are admirable. Buddhists' belief in transcendence and detachment have produced people who are, on the whole, kind and gentle, and who strive to be part of the natural processes of our planet, rather than trying to swim against the current after money and power. Until now they have espoused peace. Of course no belief remains unchanged forever, and Buddhism too has the potential to be militarized – its discipline and the way personal wants and needs are suppressed for the good of the group could still be fertile soul for violence – but so far they are an asset to the human race.

In this book I've urged you to understand that earthly material things are not important, that your body is not you, and that we will all in time become part of God and lose our individuality. In many ways Buddhism preaches the same ideals, but I have never been able to embrace the lengths to which its adherents go to reach these states of enlightenment.

Remember the little kids in their spotless, minimalist apartments in the last chapter, all wheezing or wiping drippy noses because they weren't allowed to go and root around in the sandpit? Perhaps I'm generalizing if I say that often the parents of these kinds of children are people who like order and minimalism, perhaps a Zen garden here and a koi pond there; but certainly the Buddhist ideals of non-attachment – even non-existence – seem to deny the importance of that healthy chaos in which we live. Emotions are suppressed in the eternal quest for transcendence. Sometimes it seems that Buddhists are happy because they're not showing any emotion, including happiness! It is a faith most of us could learn from – and certainly the world would change drastically if we were all Buddhists, probably for the better – but I believe there is limit to the extent to which we should live in our heads. Contemplation is fine, but life is also for living. If the pinnacle of existence is to spend all day meditating, why be here at all?

It might seem surprising to group Christianity with Buddhism, but I feel that Christianity has also moved too far towards the esoteric or abstract. Christian theology or doctrine is beautiful. It proposes a way of life that, if we could achieve it, would make our society a model of tolerance, forgiveness and hard work. For centuries its followers have been nourished by its message. Altruism and endeavour are ideas preached by Judaism and Islam as well, but in Christendom they flourished and sowed the seeds of the staggering achievements of the Renaissance and the Enlightenment.

But Christianity in practice also has a dark side, an ugly hypocrisy that at best is limiting and unpleasant, and at worst leads to self-righteous blood-letting, as in the case of the Crusades, the Inquisition and the conquest of South America. Obviously these excesses were exorcised from the faith during the Enlightenment, and today's Christianity is perhaps closer to the original teachings of Christ than ever before. And yet the hypocrisy survives, on a small, suburban scale. The priceless teachings of an extraordinary man are publicly praised but not privately emulated. Christians are taught to be charitable, but the most charitable people I know are Muslims. Christians are supposed to concentrate on living good lives with common sense, but the only people I know who live what they preach are Jews. Christians are supposed to spread their gospel, but the hardest-working evangelists I know are Hare Krishnas and Mormons.

Perhaps Christianity in the West has become too comfortable, an inescapable decadence brought about by a thousand years of prosperity. Certainly the heart and soul of the faith is no longer in Europe, or even the fervently devout United States. Africa, India and China are the new epicentres of Christendom, and it is here that the faith thrives, where the poor and oppressed who have always found refuge and hope in its message continue to reveal its merit. Christianity and Islam are religions for the poor, the lost, the forgotten. Perhaps wealth and comfort simply cannot co-exist with these faiths and leave them untainted.

I have been a Muslim in past lives, just as I have been a Christian and a Jew, but once again in this life I am on a path that doesn't embrace Islam. Not that Islam doesn't embrace me: the Koran states that Jews and Christians are Muslims too – they simply don't know they're Muslims! This is because they worship one God, and in the Muslim view, there is only one God and that is Allah. It is a very logical deduction, but as I've said, religious belief is not dependent on logic. I don't believe I am a Muslim, and I don't believe in Muslim theology. It's very kind of them to want to include me, but for now I'll go my own way.

If Buddhism and Christianity are at the more abstract end of the see-saw, then Judaism as it is practised is, in my opinion, too far towards the material side. As I've said, I'm not the first person to get pencilled in by rabbis' wives when it comes to Shabbat invitations ... But when the rabbis do deign to talk to me, it is to tackle me on my entire approach to life and belief. Why, they ask me, do I need to contact the dead, the people not in this life, since they contribute nothing to how we live? Of course I would never accuse the rabbis, who are holy men, well versed in the mystical pursuits, of being unhealthily preoccupied with material things on the earth plane. After all, they are simply preaching what Judaism teaches – to live life, and to make the best of it that you can. These teachings are honourable and admirable in a vacuum, but we don't live in a vacuum. I worry that the pressures of the modern world – ambition, materialism, an obsession with the superficial – can twist such a belief system until it finally refuses to acknowledge the higher dimensions, and tries to make a heaven on earth.

These are not criticisms of the beliefs themselves. Nearly all religious beliefs have aspects of beauty and truth and righteousness. As ideas they express the enormous godliness that we have hidden in us, and say some very reassuring things to their followers. But ideas are always damaged in practice. We are crude and clumsy. We make mistakes, and we are swayed by small emotions and petty desires. My reasons for not following the various faiths above might seem like criticisms of them, but this is not the case. Each is a path towards God. Each is steeped in complex history and fascinating doctrine. In other words, as abstract ideals they are all equally valuable. There is no hierarchy. Islam isn't better than Christianity, just as oranges are no better than apples.

However, each offers different things to souls that have chosen that specific path. Each soul seeks what it needs.

I'm getting a little abstract here, so let me cut to the chase: you go where you need to go. If, for example, you have decided to reincarnate to work through questions about how Christian belief can exist alongside scientific evidence, you will be born a Christian in the West. Another example might be a soul who needs to learn about duty and the importance of tradition, and this person might be born into a devout Muslim family in Pakistan.

Does this make evangelism pointless? If we all have the belief systems we've chosen (whether they are religious or atheist or agnostic), why bother trying to persuade people to change horses in mid-stream?

Easy. Free will. Remember, God hasn't made us as little wind-up toys and set us running along a particular groove. We are extraordinarily independent creatures, fully equipped to make our decision, both good and terrible. I'm not a fan of evangelism – and I sincerely hope that I haven't been preaching to you in this book so far! – but it is simply another choice we are faced with. Television advertisements for banks like telling us that life is all about choices, so perhaps the phrase has lost its meaning through over-use; but it is an important truth to remember. We are presented with choices all the time, and, like Grandma used to say ladling castor-oil down your throat, if it doesn't kill you it makes you stronger. So bring on the evangelists! Bring on the challenges and the questions! How else are we going to question our faith or test our belief?

Kabbalah 101

Like many people you've probably heard of Kabbalah, and developed a vague kind of idea about it. Something to do with Judaism and, well, Madonna …

If you're feeling a little left out of the loop, don't be. There's no earthly reason why you should have heard of it, or know anything about it. In fact for thousands of years people have dedicated themselves to keeping it secret!

Of course, Madonna's much-publicised conversion to Judaism in 2003, and her equally well-aired decision to study Kabbalah, promptly thrust the ancient tradition into the spotlight. As a result, most people today know the word only by association with some celebrity or another who has decided to inject some meaning and spirituality into their lives by taking up Kabbalistic studies. But Kabbalah is intrinsically secretive and fiercely mysterious. The spiritually ambivalent jet-set might have found a new accessory to try on for a while, but Kabbalah is ancient and complex enough to brush off these crude and frankly insulting approaches. Kabbalah was around long before Madonna, and it will be around long after the Material Girl and her material world have been dust for a thousand years.

What follows is a brief sketch of the basics of Kabbalah, with the emphasis on *brief*. It is simply too complex to cover in any detail in this book, and besides, this is not an appropriate forum: I'm being self-indulgent enough by inviting you to explore my own world-view, so the least I can do is to keep it brief!

But there is another more sombre reason for keeping an overview of Kabbalah short. Without wanting to sound melodramatic, there are some things that we should not be exposed to if we aren't ready for them. Kabbalah, when understood and practised with responsibility and respect, probes into the dark corners of the universe and at the same time probes into the dark places in our minds and souls, the confusing parts that we neglect. There is a very real physical and mental danger in shining a light into those parts too suddenly. Remember Pip, cast adrift on the huge, still Pacific? He is a sad but important reminder to us: madness or death awaits those who look unprotected or unprepared onto the great secrets of the universe, who glimpse the face of God.

So perhaps before I proceed, I should provide a warning: *Spiritual Surgeon General's Warning: Kabbalah can be bad for you. Kabbalah is addictive. Kabbalah will not cause cancer, but it can send you off the deep end!*

As you know, I believe it is morally and practically wrong for people who possess profound knowledge to keep that knowledge secret. Certainly Kabbalah has been carefully controlled by the rabbis (women may not teach it), and some of this restriction was as a means to entrench and guarantee their own power. But sometimes when knowledge is too complicated or would unhinge our lives too greatly, it is best left alone. I know it sounds elitist and a little hypocritical in light of the 'tell all' nature of this book, but I urge you not to pursue Kabbalistic knowledge unless you feel deeply drawn to it. If you're interested in studying it just for the sake of broadening your general knowledge or theological scope, don't. Looking for answers is important, but we all need to know what we are capable of, and what answers we can safely access.

Having said that, though, I must add the Kabbalah is self-limiting: it either resonates with you, and pulls you along through its impenetrable mazes and frustrations, or it doesn't, in which case you fall by the wayside very quickly.

In its most basic form, Kabbalah is the mystical theory on which Judaism is built. It is far more ancient than Judaism as we know it today; and you could argue that it is the original theological philosophy of the Middle East. As a result, some Kabbalists claim that it forms the basis not only of Judaism but of Christianity and Islam as well, and by implication is the spiritual foundation of both Western and Middle-Eastern culture. I don't claim to know enough, either about Kabbalah or human history, to be able to say whether this is true, but I do think that it's very likely that Kabbalah's basic myths and rituals, already so ancient and woven into society by the time of Christ and Mohammed, run deeper than most people know.

Its origins, and many of its practices, are obscure; but this is not the result of a conspiracy of silence by the rabbis or the Freemasons or any other group people like to be nervous of. The simple truth is that the history of Kabbalah is full of lost secrets and forgotten revelations. And I'm not talking about absent-minded monks laying down priceless parchments a thousand years ago en route to the vegetable patch, and then forgetting where they put them: the secrets of the universe were already being threatened in the earliest days recorded in the Old Testament.

In the beginning ...

In the beginning God created the heaven and earth, and the earth was without form and was void; and darkness was upon the face of the deep.

But ...

Before this beginning there was another, according to Kabbalah. In the beginning there was an immense, benevolent female energy, pulsing light and love and creative power. This original mother, all alone in an immense void, wanted to share Her light and love with someone or something else, and so She made a male counterpart. This new creation was part of Her and yet different, like a shoot from a single tree trunk, and together they formed a single godly entity, which for clarity I will call God.

Then, and only then, once She had made Them, did God make the universe and world and humankind and the angels. The act of creation was bound up in a great ritual, a rite that was mostly the ancient and most powerful form of Kabbalah. All the secrets of creation, of making life from nothing, were contained in that ritual and wisdom.

But there's always someone who has to spoil the party, and after a few harsh words and the odd thunderclap, Lucifer and his rebel angels were expelled from the angelic realm. But you can't keep a good artist down. Undeterred by his failure to make Man in his own image, Lucifer whistled up his posse of rebels and suggested they smuggle the secret of Kabbalah to humans on earth, to allow them to create their own paradise.

It was a strangely benevolent move by the angel we know as the Prince of Darkness, but in the end it was in vain. People being people, we didn't want to hear this new gospel, and the divine secrets went unheeded except by a small minority, who eventually died off without passing on their knowledge.

The biblical generations passed. And then, in a move unrecorded in the Christian Old Testament – and for good reason – God gave a Kabbalistic secret to Abraham. It was a brief secret, but an immense one.

It was His name, His one true name, the *Shem Hameforash*.

In the original texts of the Bible, in Hebrew and Aramaic, there are 72 names for God, but only one contains all the secrets of Kabbalah, and with them the power of creation. And it was this name – which we write as YHVH – that God gave Abraham. This verbal Kabbalah, remembered and understood intact because it had been spoken directly by God, was passed on to Isaac and Jacob, and in time to Joseph.

But Joseph died before he could pass it on himself, and for a second time humanity had to go straight to the source, as God once again bestowed the wisdom of Kabbalah (or rather, as much as people were ready for) to Moses.

These are the holy myths of the belief, but of course there are always more factual histories which take up the baton in times more recognizable and familiar than those ancient, godly days. It is commonly accepted that most of Kabbalah lore is derived from three books written by Jewish mystics between the 6th and 16th Centuries.

The first, the Sepher Yetzirah (or Book of Formation), is a short and obscure work, and usually overshadowed by the second, the Zohar or Book of Splendour, by far the longest and most famous Kabbalistic text. If Kabbalah has an Ark of the Covenant, this is it, in book form, since this was the book that kept Kabbalah intact and secret throughout the vicious onslaught of the Spanish Inquisition. Many Kabbalists were burned as heretics and sorcerers – or simply massacred without ceremony as was often the lot of Jews in those times – but their gospel survived the campaign of terror.

The third book, the Sepher Bahir, the Book of Brilliance, was written in the 1200s in Spain, and forms a profound and extremely complex link between the other two volumes. Its theology and philosophy is considerably more advanced and obscure than that found in the other volumes, and much of abstract Kabbalistic thought owes its origins to this seminal text, which seems to have been written with genius and divine revelation.

And all three are absolute gibberish.

But then, aren't coded messages always gibberish?

God in code, man in code
It's an old question, but an important one to ask and strive to answer: why would God, who apparently wants His children to

understand His advice, transmit His message in a garbled or obscure way? Why use letters and language at all? Why not simply zap the message straight into everyone's heads?

There are many answers to these questions, but perhaps the simplest is security: Kabbalah is a potent force of creation, not something to be handed out blithely to all comers. Likewise it ensures that those who seek its secrets – who battle and ponder and beg and despair and start all over again – are truly committed to its cause and authority, and not simply riding the crest of a fad.

But more importantly, it keeps predators at bay. People who exploit power for their own ends are often very determined, and will keep hacking away at an obstacle for a long time in order to get that power. But eventually they tire, because the exploitative person is by nature a lazy person. If they are powerful, they seldom won that power through hard work and the respect of their peers. If the obstacles are great enough, the paths obscure enough, these vultures will give up and go after easier prey. Only the true devotees will continue, because their own lives and ambitions are less important to them than the lore they are exploring.

The media and an endless string of conspiracy theories and B-grade action films have made us a little suspicious about codes embedded in texts. Too many authors have become too rich on our credulity, often mingling half-truth with outright fiction to grab headlines and extend their fifteen minutes of fame as long as possible.

But all texts, be they holy relics or novels or poems or shopping lists, hide clues and codes. Some codes are hidden unconsciously: our handwriting often betrays our personalities or moods. Others tap straight into our subconscious, as is the case with truly excellent poetry: the words and images distract our brains, leaving our minds unprotected and open to the poem's true meaning or impact. And still more are carefully and delib-

..ly planted, almost mechanically, to be found by those famil-
..ar with the code and its keys.

The Bible tells a story that is fairly easy to understand and
that seems straightforward. But even this apparently translucent
text is full of secrets, some put there deliberately, others accidentally. The last few years have seen a spate of books on the subject,
outlining how the original Hebrew and Aramaic seem to contain
codes, hidden there perhaps as a means of keeping their authors
safe from persecution, but also hidden to prevent unenlightened
people from abusing those secrets.

*Remember, even ancient documents with impeccable theological
histories contain alternate realities. Encoded gems or disguised
insights sit in novels, tracts, hagiographies, even devotional essays.
The answers invariably lie submerged.*

I know what you're thinking. It's all a little Hollywood, the
kind of thing Indiana Jones used to find in the jungles of
Colombia, with poison darts whizzing through his hat. But the
fact remains that we are surrounded by codes all day that we
don't see. You've already passed over one. Have a look at the previous paragraph, the one in italics. Did it seem slightly clumsy,
perhaps a little wordy? Because we aren't trained or encouraged
to look for codes, we ignore these kinds of signals. But were you
open to this slight disturbance in the flow of the writing, you
might have lingered over that paragraph. And rightly so. Write
down the first letter of each word, and what do you get?
READWITHCAREGODISINTHEDETAILS. A simple acrostic, the
oldest code in the book: '*Read with care. God is in the details*'.

Kabbalah is a great code, perhaps as close to God's meaning
and blinding truth as any code has come. It throbs with potency,
with undiscovered secrets. To those who study it, it is like an
intricate door, covered with carvings and puzzles and stories, that
stands between them and ultimate enlightenment. It is the gate-
keeper of God, the keeper of His secrets.

The Bible tells us that God created the heavens and the earth, and everything in them, but it does not tell us how He did it. Kabbalah probes into those ancient dark places, and experiments with those dangerous ingredients of creation. Again I must emphasize the dangers inherent in studying these secrets: you will know whether you are drawn to this or not, and you will also know your motives if you are. Listen to yourself before you act rashly and end up regretting it.

Qaballah, or Cabala, usually refers to the practical rites being used as high magic in the Western tradition, mostly by non-Jews who are exploiting this for the power it contains. In the Jewish tradition this ritualized use of Kabbalah – or, I should say, of bastardized forms of it – has been outlawed for centuries. Even esoteric and academic study of the discipline has been tightly restricted: the rabbis insist that you be male, older than 40, and know the Torah by heart before you are allowed to go anywhere near Kabbalah. Before this point, the rabbis insist, you are not equipped to deal with the enormous powers you might unleash.

I agree with the rabbis, but only up to a point. They might be studying a 5000-year-old discipline, but that's no reason to endorse 5000-year-old gender relations! I get a lot of stick for teaching Kabbalah and being a woman, but I take this from whence it comes: powerful old men aren't exactly the demographic most likely to encourage change and reform.

Still, there is merit in keeping the old lore sacred and secret, especially when you see the loony versions being peddled in the West. At the moment there's a particular offshoot of Kabbalah that believes in the power of osmosis. Yes, that's right: seepage. They insist that all students of Kabbalah should have a copy of the Zohar (in the original Aramaic, mind you), and that at the same time – say two o' clock on a Thursday – everyone should scan the same passage or verse. Not read (after all, what busy celebrity has time to learn Aramaic?), just look at the words as if you're staring at exotic animals in a zoo. This, according to the rabbi leading this group, is enough for enlightenment. The knowledge, the secrets of God and creation, will just seep into you.

This is pop-Kabbalah at its most infuriating, since it has added an entirely pointless aspect of magic and exoticism to something that should be worked on very hard every day *in the context of your normal life*. Gazing uncomprehendingly at Aramaic and waiting for some light-bulb to switch on simply isn't practical or logical.

The Golem of Prague

I've explained that Kabbalah contains the codes to creation, this extraordinary power that even Lucifer couldn't get away with wielding, but so far it's been an abstract idea. However, Kabbalah has a long and vibrant history of practical rites and ceremonies, and an equally long shadow history of attempted or successful abuses of this creative power. But of all the legends and histori-cally documented cases that make up the rich history of Kabbalah, the story of the Golem of Prague stands out, an eter-nal warning and an awe-inspiring reminder of the power of this secret lore.

According to myth, in 1580 the Jews of Prague were bracing themselves for fresh persecution: a rabble-rousing priest called Taddeush was planning to accuse them of yet another 'ritual murder', and bloodshed was certain to follow.

The story reached the ears of Rabbi Loeb, a scholar and teacher of the highest standing in the city, whose followers often called him 'The Exalted One'. Desperate for divine guidance on how to save his people from this constructed hatred, Rabbi Loeb asked for advice while dreaming one night. (The myth doesn't mention guides or the Halls of Learning, but clearly the rabbi was accessing higher knowledge in a way many mystics know well today.)

His answer came at once: 'Make a Golem of clay and you will destroy the entire Jew-baiting company'. But more importantly, it came with an intrinsic and secret knowledge of how to make this Golem.

J.R.R. Tolkien wasn't pulling names out of thin air when he named the wasted little creature Gollum in his *Lord of the Rings* trilogy: that character had become shrivelled over many years, gradually losing touch with its name and its soul, as its lust for the Ring grew. But Golems are a creature perhaps more dangerous and sinister. They are, in effect, zombies. They have no soul, no minds. They are empty vessels and can only do the bidding of their masters.

But in Kabbalistic lore there are few actions more illicit than creating life. Rabbi Loeb knew this, and knew that even though he was doing it to save many lives, his penalty in the afterlife would be severe. All the same, he went ahead, following the secret formula given to him in his dream. The Golem was shaped out of mud on the banks of the river Moldau, with the help of two assistants, and then sacred rites were read, and the three men performed the rituals – in this case walking around the huge shape seven times each, in opposite directions – that would bring their creation to life.

At last the massive figure began to glow with a fiery light, and when this subsided the river's water flowed through the body. Earth, fire and water had each taken their place, and finally Rabbi Loeb, despairing of his criminal act, placed a piece of parchment on the Golem's mouth which bore the *Shem Hameforash*, the true name of God, and breathed into its nostrils. The Golem opened its eyes, and they dressed it and took it back to the synagogue with them, in preparation for the work that was to come.

The story's ending varies from teller to teller, but it never ends happily. The Golem, tortured because it was alive but soulless, went mad and was destroyed; Rabbi Loeb faced his punishment. But the message is clear: use the secrets of Kabbalah to create life at your own peril.

The Tree of Life

As I have explained, to provide a 'comprehensive' outline of Kabbalah in a few pages would be a grave disservice to both the belief and to you. But no explanation, however brief, can omit the Tree of Life, one of Kabbalah's most ancient and unshakable foundations.

The Tree is as ancient as Paradise itself. It houses the serpent in the garden, it shades the first humans. But the Kabbalistic Tree of Life is not a literal interpretation of that first tree, nor do we believe, like the Norsemen, that the universe is a huge tree. It is a diagram, an analogy for the complex hierarchy of realities and realms that I have already described in detail in this book.

From the world of Malchut in the 'roots' of the tree, up through the realms we understand as real and concrete (where thought and our subconscious minds are the most abstract form of existence we can manifest), we climb towards the branches. The middle branches we recognize as the spirit world, with love and the will foremost among the branches; and finally we reach those thin, fragile, almost intangible regions at the top, the canopy, where the soul finally shucks off its physical, astral and spirit bodies, and become one with God.

For me the Tree of Life is a system of ascension, of moving from our dense earthly plane towards God. It is a great and eternal map, one that resonates with imagery and metaphor that is very powerful to humanity in general.

But whether it is a tree, or a Jacob's Ladder, or simply a long road that climbs towards a mountain top, Kabbalah is a path of enlightenment, of struggle and of discovery.

10

Kick-start your spiritual evolution

This book is about reaching out of ourselves. It's about peeping over the wall and seeing a bright new land; about recognizing that death is not the end of us. It's about looking beyond even the Hereafter, towards the bright light of God.

I have tried to tell you everything I know about what lies beyond, so that even now you can start to sense that light of hope and joy – deep inside your body, brightening like a star emerging as the dusk falls – that comes when we realize that we are not alone, that we are part of something magnificent, and that we are far more in control of ourselves than we ever thought possible.

But now it's time to turn inward, because it is only through exercising our inner minds and bodies that we can fully engage with all those treasures that wait for us outside and beyond. Each one of us has the power to go as far as we wish in this lifetime; and I hope you will take the high road, undaunted by cynicism or fear or self-doubt. It is a great road, with its vistas and serenity and overwhelming sense of acceptance, and it is reached by putting into practice much of what you have read in this book.

The meditations

The following exercises are numbered, but they are not separate. Rather they form a single meditative act that you can enter into at any time, day or night, as often as you feel comfortable with. I have broken the exercises up in this way to introduce you to them slowly, in gentle gradations, so that you aren't overwhelmed by the demands they place on you. Also, approaching them step by step is a useful way of memorizing them, so that you aren't lying on your living-room floor peeking at this book through one eye!

They are a practical way for you to start experiencing yourself as soul, to make that distinction between the material world of bodies and mass on the one hand, and the spirit world of immaterial soul on the other. If done properly, and used as part of your own personal exploration of the issues described in this book, you will be accelerating your spiritual development.

But the benefits of this programme of action aren't only limited to this life. You know now how many souls pass through death kicking and fighting, and how traumatized and disoriented they often are when they find themselves in the Hereafter. But if in life you've managed to keep a balance between the material and the spiritual – by using meditation or the exercises presented here – that transition is far smoother, and the entire experience of the Hereafter is far more fulfilling.

Before I proceed I must issue a health warning, in all earnest: people with low blood pressure should consult their doctors before doing any of the following exercises. Also if you are an epileptic, be cautious: you can feel similar to the state you are in when having a seizure. And finally, if you have ever suffered mental disorders such as psychosis or schizophrenia, don't try any of what follows: all the following exercises develop our ability to leave our reality and our bodies, and this is potentially dangerous to those who have had similar problems in this life.

What does it mean if it's not working?

If for some reason these experiences elude you, it's natural to assume that you're doing something wrong. Perhaps, if you're feeling particularly fragile, you might worry that you can't achieve these manifestations or sensations because you're being punished by God, or because you're unworthy, or something along those lines.

But: keep on trying, every day for the rest of your life. I'm guessing that like the vast majority of people on this earth, you hadn't even heard of your astral and spirit bodies, let alone tried to exercise them! If you found a new muscle today, one that you'd never used, it would be terribly weak, and you'd be frustrated in your efforts to use it. But with exercise and use that muscle will grow, until you can use it easily and with satisfying results. The same applies to these exercises. Have patience, and have stamina.

But it also doesn't matter if you don't experience anything in a literal way, because just by going through these exercises as a kind of rite has already smoothed your path in the Hereafter.

1. *Rigor vitae* – Dead and alive

This is the basic meditation, the starting point of all that follow, because it allows you to experience the sensation of being dead. It seems fairly obvious, but it's worth repeating: death is an entirely physical experience, because it only involves our bodies. Our souls – persona, personality, desires, minds – are moved from one plane to another by the death of the body, but they are not damaged or changed or altered. Mastery of this exercise will help you to understand this dichotomy, the split between body and soul, because you will experience your body for what it is: a machine, and a machine you control.

But this exercise – and indeed the others that follow – also help you to feel your aliveness. There's nothing like being in a dark room and then walking out into light to experience what sight means. Likewise feeling the weight and detachment of death will help you savour the actual sensation of being alive, with all its heat and energy and business.

Find a quiet place in your home, or go outside to a space where you can be private and detached from your surroundings. Lie flat on your back, on a yoga mat if you have one. Spread out your arms and legs so that no part of you is touching any other part. This is important, because you're trying to shut out all sensory input, to come close to a point where you're no longer sure where your body is.

Now shut your eyes, without force. Feel how heavy your eyelids are. Allow them to drop closed, with no resistance.

Most deep relaxation techniques like yoga or meditation demand that you breathe very deeply, but breath is the last thing going on when we're dead! So instead of filling your lungs, you're now going to recede and shrink, wean yourself off that primal need. Slowly, so that you don't panic, start taking shallower and shallower breaths, until your lungs are getting only what they need to keep you alive. Don't focus on your lungs or breath – you will only become claustrophobic, and distracted by the effort of starving yourself of air. Feel the faintest sensation in your throat as wisps of air slip in and out of you. Perhaps notice rhythm in your chest or stomach, now more like a slow heartbeat than the familiar rise and fall of breath.

Now feel yourself sinking into the floor. You can no longer support the weight of your body – let the floor take over. You are enormously heavy, like a sack filled with liquid lead. Feel how much effort it would take to lift your head or your arms.

And now you're beginning to feel cold. I've sometimes come out of this exercise almost blue. If you're lying in a sunbeam, or you're feeling warm, realize that these are only sensations touching your skin. Inside you are utterly immobile, and your motionlessness is draining the heat out of you. It is draining out of your head and fingers, your toes, and the tremendously heavy slab of your back, now anchored like cold granite to the floor. Feel the blood slowing in your veins, becoming sluggish and tepid.

Don't be disturbed by these sensations. You have created them from your own will and mind – you are demonstrating your mastery and transcendence over the lumpish, cold mass of your body. You are separating from it. You are reaching for something higher.

Remain in this state for a few moments. Don't count down or count your breaths – these are rhythms that imply life and motion, and you are completely still. Rather picture something moving in the world beyond you – the sun slowly coming out from behind a cloud or a twig floating past on a stream, passing rocks and reeds, until it is out of sight. If you are becoming drowsy, reject that feeling and allow the cold of your body to wake you up. Watch and wait, and allow time to pass without feeling bound to it.

Now it's time to return.

You know that you are not your body, but now feel how completely you control your body. You haven't moved it for some minutes, but you could if you wanted to. It sits around you like a sock puppet around a hand, limp and heavy, yours to control in whatever way you want. And now take a deep breath. Fill this body of yours with air (just to do it a favour!), and continue to breathe deeply. In – one – two – three; hold it – one – two – three; and out – one – two – three.

You are the master of this body, the owner and the protector, and it is yours to command. So now command it to move. First command your head and neck to move, perhaps from side to side or up and down slightly. Then your right arm and hand – be firm with them! Now your right leg and foot, and across to your left side, until finally all of your limbs are responding to your orders.

You are back, entirely fitted into your body, and working in harmony with it.

Finally get up off the floor. Move slowly, and don't force yourself if you feel a little light-headed or ill. If you still feel cold, rub your limbs and walk about, or put on warmer clothes. This cold is not spiritual or emotional – it is entirely physical and you can treat it as such.

2. Astral rising

When you feel ready to progress, whether it is a new day or weeks later, recognize that the next step towards true transcendence and spiritual awakening is to experience your 'next' body, the second-most physical casing that surrounds you. This is the astral body.

Go through the steps introduced in Exercise 1, and find yourself in that familiar territory again, with your limbs detached and heavy, your breathing shallow, and your shut eyes creating a cocoon of darkness around you.

But instead of returning to your body, visualize a bright white light, streaming in through both your closed eyes, bright enough to render the thin little membranes of your eyelids useless. Now turn your eyes to the left, and still keeping them shut, picture a dull golden light, as if a sunrise was starting away behind you and to the left. Then look up, and see a sudden explosion of purple light, like a galaxy of purple gas and stars. It streams down at you, this blazing magenta light.

Centre your inner gaze again by looking forward again in a relaxed way. Now, still lying very still, with your body starting to feel as if it is very far away and very unimportant, imagine that your skull is slowly opening down its middle, front to back, like the two halves of an observatory slowly sliding apart. The left and right sides of your head slide further and further apart, and the air in the room enters your head. It is a feeling of being exposed, of being vulnerable. But instead of retreating into these physical feelings, you swivel your eyes up. You feel the pull of the muscles and fibres at the back of your eyes, an uncomfortable pressure at the tops of your eye sockets, but you are looking up, up, up, until finally you are looking up through the top of your head into the inky blackness of the universe, of deep space.

You are locked into that vertical vision, and for a moment feel the sensation of being longer, stretched up and down like a long pillar. And suddenly your astral body begins to stir. You are a column of life right now, extending your gaze up and out of your head, your legs far away stretched downward. And like a core of light inside that column, your astral body begins to rise. Like water filling a straw it rises up from your feet. Feel it come up through you, this pillar of light inside you, sliding up through the bones of your legs, through your thighs and stomach, bursting up through the great hollow of your chest, surging up towards your neck and throat. Then it is in your head, this pressure of light and life and energy, exploding out of the open halves. Like a giant geyser it bursts out into that black sky you've been watching, shooting up into the universe. But at once it disintegrates, like the fountain it is: each fragment glints and glistens, catching the light of the other shards and flashing like diamonds in the darkness.

But this fountain doesn't stall, doesn't slow down and begin to fall back again. It continues its fractured, glinting expansion into the universe, showering the cosmos with your spirit, raining your essence up and sideways and down and through every particle of that great black space.

The first few times you do this your mind's eye and imagination will fall short. You simply can't grasp exploding your astral form all over the universe. But this will come with practice. Each time try to go further, try to burst out harder and faster. If you're struggling to break free of the shackles of imagination or your own inhibitions, try taking smaller steps: visualize yourself bursting out to cover the moon in those splinters of light. The next time race further, towards the sun; and then out, away from the sun towards the limits of our solar system. Then to a star, and then past the star, pouring over and past one, ten, a thousand stars, surging out in all directions across the universe to cover clouds of stars, swarms of blinding galaxies. You are expanding at the speed of thought through the cosmos like a blizzard of spirit, covering that glory with the fragments of yourself.

You are as diffuse as you can possibly be right now. You are spread all over the greatest distances you can imagine. But your mind is still close and compact and potent, and with a single stroke of will and focus, you gather up every spark out in the darkness, back into a single column of light. Like iron filings leaping to a magnet or spilled mercury slithering back into a single globule, every fragment springs together into the original beam that now pulses and glows out of the top of your little physical head, way down below on the earth plane.

Now it is time to re-enter the physical body, to slide the column of light back into the body, pulling it down the pillar, all the way down to the feet. Slowly, gently, allow yourself in the light to fill up that heavy sack, from the bottom to the top, again like water slowly filling up a jug. Feel the light tickling as it comes up your legs and thighs, settles into the arms, fills out the fingers like physical fingers slipping into a glove. You're now learning to clothe your astral body with your physical body.

Return to the earthly world, slowly.

3. Approaching the Halls of Learning

Surprise! Way back in chapter 5 I asked you what you'd do if you could access the Akashic Record at that moment, without having to go through the rigmarole of death and reflection and the Council. No doubt you thought this was a rhetorical question, or one that was merely illustrating a point. But I didn't say it was impossible.

Visiting the Halls of Learning while still very much anchored to the material world is a difficult skill to master. But it can be done, on a limited scale. And frankly, it should be attempted: not only is it important for us to seek divine insight into our questions and problems in this life, but it also prepares us for our post-death review before the Council, and our eventual progression through the Halls, since we will arrive with at least a smattering of knowledge about the processes we need to go through.

You've gathered up every spark you cascaded out into the universe, but now, instead of allowing your astral body to slip back into your physical body, continue to hover over your physical body. Now collect a question and hold it in your mind. You can even bring the question with you into the meditation: think of it before you enter the 'dead' state, as it can then entrench itself deeper in your mind.

Now carefully visualize the Halls of Learning – as I explained earlier, how they look is entirely up to you.

You are enclosed in your astral body, but remember that this is more of a protective layer than a living, dynamic organism. And the most striking aspect of this is that the astral body does not have eyes, just as a balaclava or helmet doesn't have eyes. But your spirit body does have eyes, and you must now look through these eyes, your vision piercing through the protective sockets of your astral body. These are the eyes that are going to expose you to everything in the Halls of Learning.

And now the will takes over. Your will has nothing to do with your mind. In fact, often it is our will that drives us when the mind has surrendered. The will is enormously strong, but we neglect it, and many of us never find it at all. But now you need to will yourself to travel to the centre of learning you have chosen. Desire it, want it, demand it, and you will arrive there at the speed of thought.

You have done enough, for now. Don't be impatient, and don't over-extend yourself. These are new and complicated 'muscles' you're finding – don't strain them. Having arrived at the doors of the great centre of learning, you must be disciplined and leave again. Withdraw your astral and spirit bodies from this place, return to the column of light, and once again fit yourself into your patient body that waits for you here, lying on its floor or mat, your little mortal home.

4. Asking

Once again leave your body, and approach the Halls of Learning. But this time enter. Let your imagination lead you to a place where you feel at home and familiar. It might be an actual seat at a table, or simply a space in a room or corridor. You can choose the same place every time you come here, until it begins to feel like a home away from home.

You are now asking your question. It is streaming out of you in the light that is shining from your spirit eyes.

There is no need to repeat your question, or to speak it aloud, or to focus particularly strongly on it once you are sure what you want to know. Very soon you will see a cloudy mist, but don't worry: this isn't a manifestation of any kind of confusion or vagueness on your part! The mist quickly clears, dissolving like smoke, and in the next instant you will experience that awesome rush of enlightenment and information that awaits us all in the Halls of Learning one day. Your question will be answered in full in a single timeless moment.

You will know when this has happened, even if the answer you sought isn't sitting comfortably and accessibly in your thoughts. You will simply feel that a kind of climax has passed, and now it is time to withdraw the light back through your eyes, back into you, and be self-contained. Now you are ready to return to your physical body, as described in the first exercise.

I said earlier that concrete, literal results aren't always achieved by these exercises, and if you re-emerge from this one without suddenly feeling like a new person with a head full of insight and wisdom, don't be disappointed or disillusioned. When you are alone and quiet, centred in stillness, you will realize that the answer has come to you. It might be while you're out walking, or in a dream, but you'll suddenly know the solution to the problem you took to the Halls of Learning.

But of course there's also the small matter of knowledge that is off limits. Remember the passwords and the Net Nanny? If you return without your answer, don't automatically assume that you've been turned away by a spiritual bouncer. But if you suspect that you have, then it's probably true! The reason for this is simple: you know, before you even ask the question, what is off limits. You know if you're chancing your luck. We all have this knowledge hard-wired into us. I had a woman come to me once who wanted to have a child but wanted to know its sex. I told her that this was seriously inappropriate, since she was effectively admitting that she was second-guessing God and the choice of her future child. And of course she understood that, although she wouldn't admit it. We know when we're overstepping the mark.

5. Strip
It is now time to slowly introduce yourself to your spirit body, and to master a meditation that will entrench in your subconscious some new empowering visualization techniques.

You have gone through the familiar stages – the 'death' of your body, the drawing together of the infinite shower of sparkling fragments, your arrival in your familiar and safe seat or room in the Halls of Learning. Perhaps until now you've simply pictured a table or bench or alcove or room, a generic and fairly vague shape. But now I want you to focus all your attention on what this place looks like. If it's an alcove, is it private or open to passers-by? How high is the ceiling? Is it a modern building or an ancient, sun-baked ruin of an amphitheatre? What does it smell like? What do you hear? Clocks ticking? Doves calling quietly to each other? The rush of the sea somewhere close by? Look around inch by inch until you have a fixed picture of your space.

However it looks, this place is entirely sympathetic and safe. Here you are free to be yourself and learn whatever you are able. And this is the place you will return to each time you come here. It is your 'den' in the Hereafter.

Now see yourself standing in this space, free and alone, touching no walls or furniture or anything else you might have created in the space. Look down, and you will see a beautiful glistening golden cloak. Pick it up. It is incredibly light; in fact it has no weight at all, and you realize it is made of silky, incredibly thin strands like spiderweb. It is very soft.

Feeling its softness on your fingers and neck, sling it around your shoulders and let it hang down to your thighs. You've never worn a cloak before, or at least not one this exquisite, so just enjoy the sensation of regality and dignity for a moment.

Now take it off. Feel how it slips off your neck and shoulders, and finally hangs from your fingers. Let it drop to the floor.

You have made this golden cloak from thought. You have imagined it, seen it with your mind's eye, and created it for you to put on and discard in your special safe place. And now it's time to make something else: a golden robe. Hold it up before you, and stroke the silkiness of its long sleeves, feel the strain in your shoulder as the weight of the body-length robe drags at your arm. Now slip it on, feeling your hands and arms slipping down the sleeves, the cool smooth weight of it hanging down your back, its soft hem brushing your ankles. And once again, take it off, and let it drop down next to you.

You are naked, but you don't know what you look like in this form. You have never seen yourself as you are. But now you see a mirror on a small table next to you, a small mirror but one that is big enough to see parts of you in. Look into the mirror, and without picking it up, tilt and shift it in such a way that you can see your eyes. It is a startling sight: your eyes are filled with light. Not a demonic glow, but a clear, sparkling luminescence that radiates gentleness and wisdom. You realize you have already seen something like this, in the material world, in the eyes of those you love. You've seen the light in their eyes every time they've walked into a room and met a friend, or been happy or excited.

Then move the mirror another fraction, and see your face. It is familiar and ordinary, but at the same time entirely changed, as if you were looking at an old friend you haven't seen in years. Here too there is an inner glow, an actual pulsing of light, that fills you with awe and wonder at the beauty of your own spirit and those in the material world around you.

Energised by this vision, you look down at your arms and at the rest of your body; and for the first time you see through the thin skin of light that covers you. Under this gently glowing covering you see thin threads of bright white light, sitting just under the surface. Remember, this is not a body. There are no organs or bones, just energy coursing through what you can visualize as a kind of nervous system. It runs through you like a network of light.

Admire these little glowing, pulsing tributaries, and see how they fork and intertwine under your skin. But now they are moving more decisively, and becoming brighter. They are rising up towards the outer skin, reaching for the world beyond you. Allow the threads to flow up through your skin. There is no sensation attached to this experience, no pain or tingle, just wonder at seeing these beautiful skeins of light emerging from you.

Allow them to emerge a little way, and feel the sense of becoming enlarged and enlivened by these new 'feelers'. But this is enough for now. Watch them for a while, marvel at their beauty and their potential for constant growth, the way they branch and branch as if they are striving to be connected with everything in the universe. But then gently will them to recede back under your golden skin, until they return to their original positions, where they glow under the surface as veins of light.

Practise this meditation for as long you wish, and become accustomed to these tendrils of light. Become familiar with the manifestation of sending them out of your body to touch and feel the space around you, of exerting your will and quiet mastery of them by drawing them back into you.

Finally, focus once more on your quiet space in the Halls of Learning, find your cloak and robe on the ground next to you, your familiar seat a few paces away. Be still in this safe place for a few moments, and then once again return through the phases to your physical body.

6. Transcending form

You are standing naked and beautiful in your spirit body, enjoying the sensation and sight of sending your light feelers out through your golden skin and drawing them back again; watching fascinated at their slow and steady movements as they try to make connections with each other and the space around you.

In this meditation, send them out again, but this time don't draw them back into you. Wait and watch, and allow them to continue out in their gently probing way.

And suddenly they begin to dissolve, like rivulets of silver sinking into sand; but instead of disappearing they become a fine bright mist, and simultaneously your golden skin – this body you have manifested – also begins to melt, merging with the mist of light seeping from you.

Don't be alarmed or confused by the smoky dissolution going on around you. You are never separate from your various elements. Even though you seem to have split into two distinct substances, they are mingled and merged, almost indistinguishable as the threads of light weave and split and join through the golden mist of your dissolved spirit body.

And now you must realize what has happened: your body is long gone, and by earthly standards you are completely nebulous. Even these misty, intangible substances in which you now exist seem to be diffuse and unreal. But you are still you. You haven't evaporated or dissolved. This is the ultimate manifestation, the ultimate confirmation, that you are not your body. Soul and physical shape are not linked. Understand this now, through meditating and perfecting these exercises, and your progression in the Hereafter will be speedy and rewarding.

7. Manifesting form

You have let go, and have marvelled at the confluence of matter and non-matter in the beautiful, softly glowing mist that is your new phase. But now it is time to reassert your will – the will of the spirit and soul – over physical matter: it is time to mould this amorphous mass back into the shape of the body.

Decide that you want to be a body again, but remember that you can be any body. Our bodies are merely tools, random shapes decided by the coin-toss of genetics and material events. There is nothing mystical or eternally beautiful about a particularly attractive or shapely body, despite what Greek sculptors and personal trainers might think! So choose whatever body you want, be it human or anything else, and be very firm in your decision about wanting to appear in that form.

Just as when the will snapped up all the millions of fragments of astral body in the first exercises, so it now snaps these diffuse mists together into the shape of the body you have chosen. It happens as quickly as thought, and is as dramatic and decisive as the act of making a decision. You know that feeling: the resolve that suddenly galvanizes you. The sudden forming of a body is that resolve made visible or tangible. Like smoke wrapping itself into a concrete shape, like water suddenly freezing into a particular form: this is how the diffuse becomes the tangible.

You are now back in your light body, with a new understanding of how changeable it is, and how powerful we can be in shaping ourselves. Look at it again in the mirror, to drink in this understanding, and remember how easy and how natural it felt to dissolve, to move around as a mist of light, and then how easy it was to take on a shape again: these memories will remain with you in the heavy, demanding material world, and will make the conceits and obsessions of this world seem a little less important. As before, return to your astral body and then your physical body.

8. Dressed for success

This is a short meditation, and, compared with the previous one, fairly easy. But it is important because it is the next logical step in the process of learning how to manifest from thought.

You have learned how to clothe yourself in any body you choose in this non-material world, and you have experienced the sensation of manifesting or creating that body; but now you need to complete this creative process. There is one thing missing from this picture: clothes.

Of course you don't need clothes – they are an entirely material creation, invented to protect us from material concerns. But they are a useful tool in learning to manifest whatever you want, since we all know clothes so intimately, and know exactly what we like about them.

You've made a body, so this should be a doddle. All the same, think very clearly about what clothes you'd like. Imagine their cut and their weight, their smell and texture. If they are made of silk, feel that soft slippery sensation of silk sliding across your skin as you put it on. Is it linen, with its lumpy, cool texture? Feel it on your skin, all over you. Feel where it doesn't touch your skin, perhaps where it hangs loose over the small of your back. Imagine touching your sleeves, rubbing the fabric between thumb and forefinger. Look at yourself in your new clothes, and enjoy the sensation of being well dressed. It makes you feel compact, capable, free.

9. The easel – a home between homes

You've made a body, clothed it, but you've not yet created an entire reality for yourself. Your creations have been personal and internal, but now it's time to project your creative power out into the universe.

Go to your den, your safe place, and you will find an artist's easel with a large clean canvas on it, primed and ready. Your paints lie next to it, every colour you could want, and you have a range of brushes to choose from.

Now paint a home for yourself.

Don't hold back. Don't employ standard worldly excuses and explanation: I'm not a painter, I can't draw, it'll look ridiculous, look what a mess I'm making. None of these things are valid here. From the moment you touch brush to canvas, you realize that you are drawing out a line of paint so perfectly textured, so clean and full of expression, that those petty concerns seem a universe away.

As you focus on the details of your home – fascinating nooks, a sense of light and space, perhaps the comforting and calming presence of lots of dark wood, a garden of sunlight and shade – the painting seems to come to life. Light glints off the window panes, and a breeze seems to ruffle the curtains and sets the flowers under the window bobbing slightly. And slowly the canvas becomes longer and wider, and the image becomes clearer, the colours crisper, and suddenly you are certain about that breeze on your cheek, and that hint of a laugh from beyond the kitchen door. Your canvas has become a window onto a real home, one that exists independently of your brushes. You dab here and there, but your additions are now only slight alterations to this concrete place you have manifested through thought and intention. The paints distracted you from over-thinking it, and kept your hands and eyes busy. Your mind was thus freed to focus entirely on something it wanted to create, and this peaceful murmuring home was the result.

Now step through the window. Look back and see the frame, see the vague shapes of your special place in the Halls of Learning. But the sun is warm on your neck, and the flowers in the garden smell like home, and you turn to look for the source of the voices that you are now hearing. And coming out to meet you, stepping down the garden path and waving out of the windows of this home, are those you have loved and missed, those who have died. Your parents, if they are dead, come to you, each walking in their distinctive way, Mother in front like always, or Dad stopping for moment to pull up his sock or toss an unwanted snail off the path as was always his habit. Perhaps it is an old friend you have found, smiling that unforgettable smile or yelling out a silly greeting that the pair of you always used to get hysterical over. You are overjoyed as you hold them close, and it is with a deep sense of gratitude and satisfaction that you invite them into your home where they have been waiting for you. Finally, in manifesting this home in which spirits in the Hereafter can stay, you have created common ground. Through earthly meditation, you have created a space between you and the Hereafter that you and these loved ones can enter and in which you can share each others' company. It is like a beautiful and joyful border post between two countries: belonging to neither, a temporary and transitory place, but one where people can meet as equals without ties to time or space.

10. Touching spirit

The keenest aspect of grief is not being able to touch those we have lost. We long to be able to hug them one last time, or to stroke those faces that we know so well. We want to hold their hands and feel their health and warmth and strength, and we want to feel their arms around us, to know that they love us as much as we love them.

And now we can.

The titanic act of manifesting a halfway-house between our world and theirs has fulfilled that great yearning of ours. And now, as you enter this deepest and most profound meditation, it is time to learn how it feels for you in your astral skin to touch those you love in their spirit bodies.

You have manifested the home, and all its beautiful surroundings, and you're also in that twilight state between actual experience of your astral body and manifestation or visualization brought on by this series of meditations. But you are not manifesting the appearance of these spirit bodies. They are here, of their own free will and out of love for you, and they have gathered their own amorphous, golden beings into a spirit body for your benefit. They are beautiful and glowing, but nonetheless they have condescended to assume those old shapes, with those familiar faces, that you know and love so well.

But however 'real' a spirit body looks, it can never feel 'real'. Reach out to them with your hands, and see how they smile and draw closer. And now touch their hands or faces. This is no skin that you remember, no soft cheek or stubbly jaw. The skin of their spirit bodies – this covering they have so kindly manifested – feels to you like flowing water, like rushing air, and as you hold them you yourself feel that you and they are flowing together. Next time you are running a tap hold your hand under it and close your eyes to feel the sensation of flow. Not wetness or cold or force, just flow. This is the overwhelming sensation you experience now as your astral body touches their spirit body.

Feel your body, its limits and boundaries, and through the flow feel theirs and their limits. Feel how irrelevant those boundaries have become in this rushing interchange of senses. Feel their love for you, swirling across you.

But you can't stay in the halfway house for long, and neither can they. This is not the reunion in the Hereafter that follows our death. This is a temporary window opened by you using your will and the power of visualization. Allow them to return to their lives beyond the veil, and return to your own, slowly coming back through your head and into your human body in the way you are now familiar with.

11. The final hurdle – shucking the astral body

You have slowly learned how to experience the death of your physical body. You have learned how to leave that body behind via your astral body. You have travelled to that safe haven of yours in the Halls of Learning, a kind of spiritual studio where you are free to learn and experiment, and where you are safe enough to see your spirit body finally reflected in the mirror. Through the meditations above you have allowed your spirit body to become diffuse; you have seen the beauty of those tendrils of light that run like a great nervous system through you. And you have manifested a tranquil halfway house in which the spirits of your loved ones feel safe and welcome enough to visit you, even though you are not physically dead and have not yet passed over into their world.

Now only one experience is left to us in this meditation, and it is an act that is potentially extremely dangerous. Again, I must stress that people with a history of mental illness must not try this. Because what you are now going to experience – just for a moment – is the stripping away of the astral body and casting it aside.

You will die if there is nothing animating your body. I'm talking here about a physical death: you'll flatline, croak, kick the bucket. Our astral body is part of this animation; so obviously we can't toss it away entirely or walk away from it. But we can let it hover close enough to us that the trauma of that separation does not cause us any physical harm.

The spirit body clothes the soul, like the enamel of a tooth around a raw nerve. It is what contains our persona or personality, and it acts out our karma through many human lifetimes. But if the spirit body is the clothing of the soul, what is the astral? How can we visualize this nebulous yet strangely concrete body?

Well, think of rubber. Or more specifically, a wetsuit. If the 'clothing' provided by the spirit body is made of the finest silk and linen, then a heavy, sweaty and tough suit like a wetsuit seems the ideal description of the astral. But it's appropriate in another important way: your astral 'clothing', like a wetsuit, is very difficult to take off!

Reach the state of Exercise 2, with your head opened and your astral body rising up to your head like a cylinder of light; but don't explode out into the cosmos. Stop your astral body as it reaches your head or neck, and visualize now how you peel it down off you, like an unzipped wetsuit. It is awkward and slow, and it clings to you, but you push and pull and wiggle from side to side, and gradually you roll and peel it down. At last your feet come free, and you step out. But allow the astral body, now suddenly as fragile and delicate as a discarded snakeskin, to float just above you.

Now allow your beautiful spirit body to blaze out in all its glory, and roll your spirit eyes down into your own body. If you are very lucky you will experience yourself in this incarnation, and see yourself as soul. You will come as close as is possible in this world and the next to knowing yourself as you are, and no-one can return from that experience unchanged. When you return to your physical body and go about your daily business, everything will have changed because you will have changed. You will be unable to pollute yourself with unhealthy ideas or unhealthy food; you will no longer undermine yourself as we all do in the material world, because you will have caught a glimpse of your own glory; and you will find new and intense respect for all others because they too are soul.

This is a staggering state to achieve, but it comes with material dangers. I must stress that you must never attempt this final exercise alone: the others can be performed alone or with a partner, but should you make this final breakthrough on your own, and taste this nirvana, it is possible that you will refuse to return to the dullness and ignorance and pain of the material world, and stay, disembodied and lost in meditation, on the spirit level. I often lead these guided meditations in Kabbalah classes, and I've seen how people return out of their deep meditative states glowing with ecstasy; but often they report that the next day was very hard on them, as the harsh realities of this world were thrown into depressing contrast by the wonderful state they had entered.

So now you are standing in your spirit body, with the discarded astral floating close by. Centre your gaze straight ahead, and feel what it is like to have a spirit body. It seems to flame constantly, with a rushing like the ocean or wind. Now you need to move away from your physical and astral bodies, in order to be totally free. Even the Halls of Learning and your secret place there are too constricting now – you want to travel at the speed of light, and go beyond anything your astral body has led you to before.

And as you stand in the inky blackness, a hole opens up – a wormhole, a tear, a gateway, call it what you will – and you are pulled towards it, faster and faster. Feel yourself being sucked through it, and listen to the rushing of the flame and the surging of distance as you sweep through this passage between universes.

Suddenly you are blind, your eyes seared by the brightest of all lights. You have arrived somewhere, but where you cannot tell, because the light is making all sight impossible. Do not look at the light, or try to guess what its source is. Instead look down, down into your spirit body. I can't describe here what you'll see, but if you see your soul, then you won't need this book any more. In fact you won't need very much at all any more.

But as suddenly as you were pulled through to this place with its godly, blinding light, you are being pulled away again, back to the place you stood, back to your little astral body waiting patiently like a faithful hound. And as you come closer it raises itself up to you, and as you stand still again, it reattaches itself to you, sliding down over and through you. You are encased once more, safe and snug, and you can re-enter your physical body to take up your life once again.

Finding the immaterial in the concrete

The meditations above are a means to an end. They should not be used as tools to boost your self-esteem, or a form of worship in themselves. Like any exercise they are designed to be repeated many times, to develop skills that will help us in the long term.

I hope you find the time and motivation to work your way slowly through them until you have a reached a point where their sensations and lessons come to you as second nature. But it is also important, as with any course of study or exercise, to step back every so often, to evaluate where you are and what it is you're doing.

Stop, and ask yourself three simple little questions.

Firstly, have you become aware that you are spirit and not flesh?

Secondly, have you found a way of finding stillness? Do you have a special place, either in this world or in a manifestation of the Halls of Learning, where you can see and hear clearly, undisturbed by material or emotional concerns?

And thirdly, are you slowly becoming aware that you are part of a higher power, a being far greater than you?

This third question is the core of everything I have covered in this book. It is the great question of this age, and almost every age before it. And it is a question fraught with doubt and longing, because when you come right down to it, we want proof. We have always wanted proof, yearned for an apparition or a revelation or a miracle. We must not criticize or belittle ourselves as petty or superficial because we want these things. Rather we must accept that our desire for proof comes from our intellect, our reason, which is one of God's most glittering gifts to us.

But our search for proof is deeply personal and private. Other people's miracles are nothing more to us than frustrating gossip. Perhaps you bought this book as part of that search for proof, but as you already know there's nothing I can tell you that will make you really believe. You must find your own proof. It's the eternal quandary of faith and belief: it's not a matter of persuading. You believe, or you don't. You've seen the burning bush, or the vision on the road to Damascus, or the huge vastness of the Universe as you've floated alone in the sea; or you haven't.

But even if you have had your revelation, the search for God is not over. Some evangelical faiths suggest that all it takes is to experience that moment. This can be a dangerous belief when you've got a hall full of unfulfilled people, desperate for hope and love, and willing to part with any amount of money to get it. And of course, even the most rational, cynical people can be swept up in a moment. No, the flash or revelation or moment of clarity is just the start. It's what makes you realize that you need to be asking questions. Then you have to figure out the question, and if you're very very lucky, you might get one or two answers over the course of your life.

But if it was meant to be easy, we'd be born with couches attached to our rears. Keep searching. Keep questioning. And always return to the silence, to the still darkness, to step up and peer over the wall into that other country that we all long for.

11

The future

Before us lie an infinite number of paths, each known by God. Many of them are daunting, with complex moral and social issues: our world is not the simple, practical place it was just two hundred years ago. Our planet is sinking under our relentless consumption of space and resources. This too will be reversed, but the upheavals will be enormous, their shockwaves rippling around the world.

We in the West will become increasingly removed from these problems, as our governments and media scale up their huge campaigns of denial and misinformation, while they work feverishly at putting up a dyke of technology and money between us and the millions of destitute human beings scraping out an existence in the developing world. Eventually even these walls will fall, because for every action there is an equal and opposite reaction. Revolutions, erasing of borders, new corruptions and new endeavours of heroism and altruism: all will come.

But even this cocoon of privilege that awaits us in the West will be beset with complex psychological and spiritual obstacles. The first will be the evolution of a robotic worker-caste, given intelligence but not free will, a race of machines bred into slavery. As we become used to being masters, so the old lines of right and wrong will blur. After all, people are much more useful than machines; and with four fifths of the world's population clamouring to work for the crumbs on our tables, how soon will robotic slaves give way to human ones?

Then will come the era of the new Golems, humanoids combining biology and technology, given life and free will. But only God can ensoul. Clones have souls, because they have the God code, the basics of Kabbalah, in their DNA; but these constructed creatures will be nothing more than zombies, and then Man will have stepped into Lucifer's shoes, setting himself up as God's competition.

And finally, the ultimate human catastrophe: the end of death. Nanotechnology will advance to the point when cell-sized robots repair us constantly, improve us every day. Our minds, linked to infallible computer systems controlled by all-powerful corporations, will be like those of angels: filled with all knowledge but simultaneously entirely incapable of independent thought. They will never fade or fail. We will be the Immortals our ancestors wrote stories and songs about.

But some human realities you can't delete from a hard-drive, and poverty will remain. The rich will live as long as they want, the poor will die, and the resentment of the vast majority will be intense and awful. There will be wars, civil wars, great plagues of murder and revolution; but the poor will always lose to the rich.

It is a bleak picture. But stand back for moment and ask yourself this: when, in our history, has the picture not been bleak? Would you have wanted to bring a child into the world in 1960, with the threat of nuclear war? In 1941, with Nazism apparently set to rule the world? In 1916, with the so-called civilizations of Europe surrendering to butchery in the trenches of the First World War? In 1800, with wars of colonization and territorial aggression obliterating nations and cultures on six continents, with smallpox and leprosy spreading unchecked and education a distant dream for most people? Or what about the Middle Ages, with barbarism, plague and religious fanaticism rampant across the world?

The reality of our world, this turbulent little ball of mud we live on, is that people hate and fight and misunderstand. But people also love and hope and reach out to God, despite everything; and this courage will not fail us. The light of humanity will not be dimmed. Greater challenges simply mean greater rewards. The future lies before us like our blank canvas. God is as far away as He's ever been, but He's also never been closer. God remains constant, and will always do so.

How will you face the future? How will you define this life? Will you continue to live as a good father or mother, husband or wife, scholar or teacher, or will you no longer be content with simple goodness, and begin the slow journey towards God?

Don't be afraid, and don't be confused. You've lived a human life many times before, and answered your own questions over and over again. God is waiting.

But first, life is waiting.

Acknowledgements

I am deeply grateful to Tom Eaton who helped me get my thoughts down on paper, and also to all at Double Storey Books who have made this book possible.

I honour and thank the many people, living and on the other side, for the knowledge and experience I have gained through my interactions with them.